THE
Essential
QUILTER
PROJECT BOOK

THE
Essential
QUILTER
PROJECT BOOK

20 projects from the author of the
best-selling *The Essential Quilter*

━━━━━━

BARBARA CHAINEY

Photography by Roger Brown

David & Charles

A DAVID & CHARLES BOOK

First published in the UK in 1997

Text and designs Copyright © Barbara Chainey 1997
Layout Copyright © David & Charles 1997
Photography Copyright © Roger Brown 1997

ISBN 0 7153 0485 2

Book design by Maggie Aldred
Page make-up by Les Dominey
and printed in Italy by New Interlitho SpA
for David & Charles
Brunel House   Newton Abbot   Devon

CONTENTS

Introduction
7

Chapter One
Tools and Techniques
8

Chapter Two
Traditional Wholecloth
Quilting
22

Chapter Three
Trapunto and Corded
Quilting
50

Chapter Four
Machine Quilting
63

Chapter Five
Sashiko and Kantha
Quilting
79

Chapter Six
Quilting with Patchwork
and Appliqué
94

Chapter Seven
From the Antique
122

Selected Bibliography
142

Acknowledgements
143

Index
144

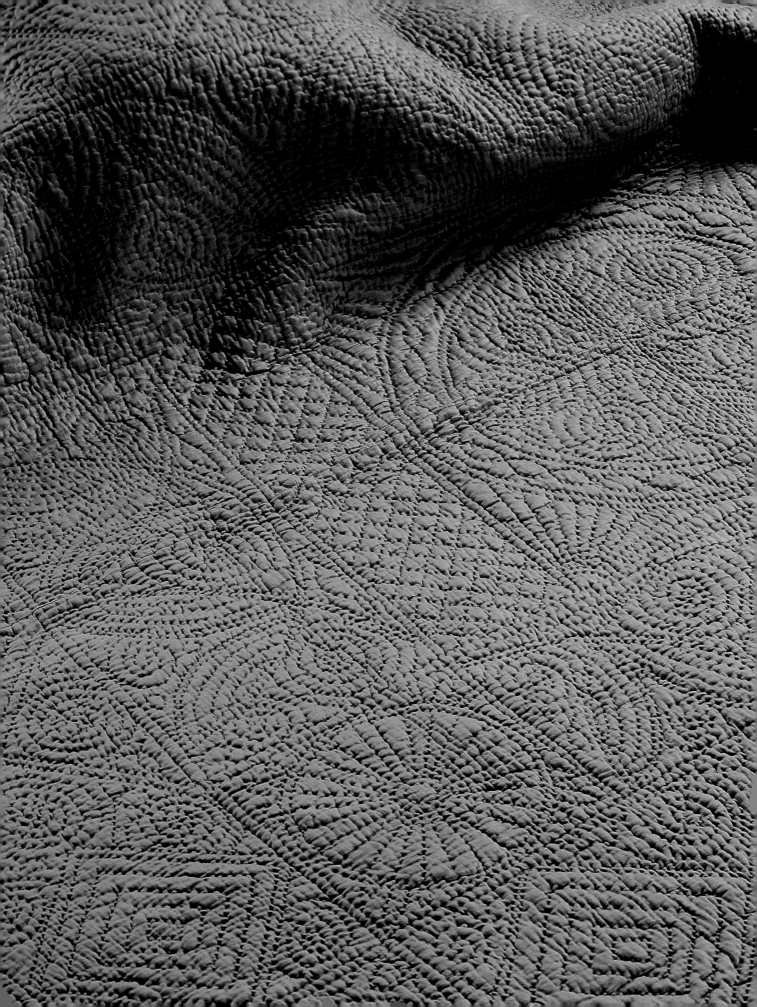

INTRODUCTION

Several lifetimes ago *The Essential Quilter* came into being, and since then it has been my pleasure to meet and teach hundreds of quilters of all levels of experience. Teaching is indeed its own reward. I continue to learn from these students as much, if not more, than they learn from me, and for this I am very grateful. However, teaching and talking to quilters also continues to confirm my already 'strong views' on quilting and, if you missed them first time around, here they are again. First, quilt. Worry about the quality of your quilting once you have done quite a lot of it. Good quilting is what happens after lots of practice and you relax and enjoy the process for its own sake. If how you are quilting feels right for you and gives you a good result, stop worrying that someone else is doing it differently – there is no one True Path to quilting excellence. After fifteen years or more, I'm still in love with quilting and I hope that this book will make you feel the same.

HOW TO USE THIS BOOK

I hope you will enjoy dipping into the different quilting techniques described in the following pages – traditional quilting in Chapter Two, corded quilting and trapunto in Chapter Three, the wonder of the modern age, machine quilting in Chapter Four, quilting from the East in the form of sashiko and kantha in Chapter Five, quilting with patchwork and appliqué, Chapter Six; and back to traditional quilting, but on a large scale, in Chapter Seven. No technique is more complicated than any other, but all require a modest amount of practice before you will feel comfortable with the process. The projects in each of the chapters are therefore presented in order of ascendancy, beginning with the simple and progressing to the more complex. Even if you are new to quilting in any form, the majority of the projects are well within your capabilities and you will find practical information on marking, equipment, construction techniques, finishing, labelling and quilt care in Chapter One. Experienced or improving quilters have not been forgotten – why not try out a new

technique or launch into a full-size quilt such as those in Chapter Seven? If you have never tried machine quilting but always meant to, the projects in Chapter Four are especially for you – having been a committed handquilter for years, I have finally 'seen the light' as regards machine quilting, and if I, with my non-technological inclinations, can now feel relatively at ease when quilting by machine, then so can you.

All of the patterns shown in the projects are original to their makers – enjoy using them for yourself, but please remember the usual rules of acknowledgement that we have come to regard as courteous.

The fabric requirements for each of the projects in this book have been calculated with a distinct generosity of spirit. I take no pleasure from cajoling something out of 'only just enough', preferring instead to have some fabric left over for another day or another project. In any event, quilters need to support the hopes of the fabric industry world-wide, which is looking to us to buy far more than we need.

CHAPTER ONE

Tools and Techniques

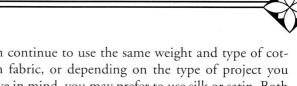

Hand quilting requires few specialist tools or equipment to begin with. As you go along, you may acquire numerous extra gadgets and gizmos but the basics are relatively inexpensive, easy to find and will last a long time.

Fabrics

Theoretically it is possible to quilt with almost any fabric although very heavy, thick or closely woven fabrics present obvious difficulties for stitching and handling. If you come to quilting via patchwork or appliqué, you will probably be quilting on the dress-weight cottons which are the most popular choice for both of these techniques. For wholecloth quilting you can continue to use the same weight and type of cotton fabric, or depending on the type of project you have in mind, you may prefer to use silk or satin. Both require more careful handling than cotton, as they are more fragile and mobile and less easy to mark with a pattern. Quilting does wonderful things to fabric and you do not have to use a fancy fabric to create a stunning effect.

Scissors and rotary cutters

You need a minimum of two pairs of scissors – one should be reserved for fabrics only, jealously guarded and kept out of general view, the other pair kept in your sewing basket for snipping threads. A pair of

scissors for cutting paper, cardboard and template material will also be useful but be sure not to mix them up with your fabric scissors. Buy the best you can afford and look after them. Rotary cutters together with their companion rulers and self-healing mats are considered by many quilters to be as basic and just as essential as scissors – armed with a rotary cutter and mat you can cut up more fabric more quickly and with more accuracy than you would ever have imagined possible. None of the projects in this book depend on your owning a rotary cutter but you are sure to find one useful if you do decide to buy one.

Batting

Nowadays there is a bewildering choice of battings (also known as waddings) available – cotton, cotton/polyester, polyester, wool, silk – in an equally bewildering variety of thicknesses from featherlight to downright chunky. You won't go far wrong in choosing a standard 2-ounce polyester batting for most projects until you feel the need to experiment with some of the other types. The dramatic increase in popularity of machine quilting has resulted in an ever-widening selection of thin, densely textured needlepunched battings which are easy to machine but less suitable for hand quilting.

Preparation of battings

In the early days of the quilting revival (somewhere in the 1970s), it was difficult to find any batting other than polyester, which required no preparation before use and generally performed well. Over the last twenty years the choice of battings has increased almost beyond belief and some of the cotton battings in particular need some preparation to make quilting easier. Please read and observe the manufacturer's recommendations in order to get the best from a particular batting. Above all, note that wool battings generally require **no** preparation before quilting – horror stories abound of quilters who have inadvertently reduced a beautiful (and expensive) wool batting to shreds of felt because they thought that this type of batting should be pre-washed or pre-rinsed.

Marking

This is undeniably seen by many as one of the 'problem' areas of quilting. How do you get the pattern onto the fabric before beginning to quilt? Will the marks come out easily? What is the best marker to use? Is there a right way to mark?

There are a number of ways of marking a pattern onto fabric (of which more anon); there is no single right way to mark fabric, there is no single marker which outperforms all others, and the ease with which marks are removed depends entirely on the type of marker used. Let's begin with a simple rule – one of the very few in quilting. It is up to you to test any marker for ease of use and removal from the fabric, irrespective of anything you may have been told about that particular marker or any previous experience you may have of its use. The more you experiment with different markers and marking methods, the more likely you are to develop your own preferences. You just need to be aware of the choices available to you and remember to test for ease of removal before marking up a complete project.

Pencil

This is a tried and tested marker which has been used for marking by generations of quilters. It requires a lightness of touch and a well-sharpened point and testing before use.

Chalk

Tailor's chalk gives a relatively broad line which rubs off easily but there are several chalk wheels available which give a fine line which withstands limited wear before disappearing.

Washout and fadeout pens

These are easy to use and the lines are visible on most fabrics. Work marked with a washout (or water-soluble) pen requires that the work is soaked in cold water for successful removal despite assurances that the lines can be sponged or sprayed away after quilting. Partial wetting may result in an unwelcome tidemark reappearing later. Do not expose any work marked with this type of pen to direct heat, such as ironing, which may set the pigment into the fabric and be virtually impossible to remove.

The fadeout (or air-soluble) pen should be used only with the greatest of caution – the lines may fade before you have finished quilting and the chemicals which allow the lines to fade may have a detrimental effect on fabric in the long term.

Soap and soapstone

Leftover slivers of soap make excellent temporary markers if they are first air-hardened. By their very nature they can easily be washed out of the finished piece. Soapstone is now available in pencil form and gives a pale mark which is easily brushed off.

Crayon and pastels

Water-soluble (or painting) pencils and artist's pastel pencils can be excellent markers if used lightly and pretested for ease of removal. It is often possible to brush out the marks of pastel pencils and to sponge out lines from the water-soluble type. Both have the advantage of being available in a wide range of colours, which means that you can choose a shade which is just slightly darker than the fabric you will be marking.

Patterns, templates and stencils

After you have chosen and tested your marker, you still have to put the pattern onto the fabric. By now you will not be surprised to learn that there are a number of ways of doing this and that no single method will be right for every fabric and occasion.

For many quilting patterns you can make a template by tracing the shape you want, gluing the tracing onto card or plastic and cutting carefully around the outside of the shape. Mark around the template directly onto the fabric; this gives you the outer shape only and any additional lines are added freehand. Many quilters blench at the word freehand and immediately feel that this is beyond them as they 'cannot draw'. Again it is that magic ingredient practice which will give you the confidence to do this – try drawing around the template onto paper first and then filling in extra lines, and you'll be surprised at how easy it can

be. Stencils are even easier to use than templates because they enable you to mark all the lines and connect the small gaps once the stencil has been removed and there is a huge variety of commercial stencils to choose from.

Tracing

Of course, you could always cheat a little by marking your chosen quilting design onto tracing paper using a medium black marker pen and laying the tracing on a smooth surface with a sheet of white paper slipped underneath it. If your fabric is light in colour you should be able to see the black lines on the tracing through the fabric when it is taped into position over the tracing. Remember to check that you have traced all the lines of the pattern before lifting the fabric off. If your fabric is too dark for this method to work, put the tracing on a window, glass-topped table, or light box so that there is a strong light behind or underneath it and you should find that the pattern is sufficiently visible through the fabric for you to trace the lines with a light-coloured marker.

Masking tape

If you want to quilt simple straight lines, strips of masking tape laid on top of the quilt will give you a clean straight edge to quilt against without needing to mark out all the lines beforehand. Do not leave masking tape in position for any length of time or you may

Marking a quilt top using templates and stencils.

Tracing a pattern through thin, pale-coloured fabric.

find that it leaves a sticky residue which can be tricky to remove. Be wasteful in your use of tape and use each piece once only to ensure the straightest possible edge to guide your quilting. It is possible that you will find it easier to quilt accurately along the upper edge of the tape rather than the lower, or perhaps that is just one of my personal preferences. Quarter-inch (5mm) width masking tape is a popular choice for many quilters, but take care if you want to use it to quilt lines which are ¼ inch (5mm) apart. It simply does not stick to fabric well enough to be a truly accurate guide and you may find that you spend more time trying to press it back down than actually quilting. You may find it simpler to use a wider tape as a guide, measure the required distance and position a fresh piece of tape to indicate the quilting line.

Stitch and tear

For nervous machine quilters much of the thorny issue of what to use and how to mark can be resolved by using paper sheets which have the pattern printed or marked on. Pin or baste the sheet to the work and then is simply follow the marked line and tear away the paper when the stitching is complete. There is no good reason why you should not use this method for hand quilting, except that handstitching through paper can be awkward.

Making a Master Sheet

This is a grand-sounding term which simply means that you plan a quilting project in its entirety before doing anything else. You can use tracing, greaseproof or ordinary white paper for this – the translucence of tracing paper may be helpful if you want to mark dark fabrics over a light box. For a small project of say 36 inches (91cm) or less, it is fairly straightforward to have the Master Sheet show the complete design (Fig 1), whereas for a large quilt of symmetrical design it may be less cumbersome to make a Master Sheet of just one quarter of the area (Fig 2).

Even if you do not plan to use the tracing through method of marking, there are advantages to taking the time to make a Master Sheet. Most of us find it reassuring to see a design fully drawn out before putting it onto fabric. It also gives a clear reference should you need to re-mark any part of the design at a later stage, or if you will be using mainly templates to mark the design. It also offers the opportunity to try out various ideas for background quilting before committing them to stitch. Of course, if you have the confidence to draw your design directly onto the fabric, do just that, but you might like to make a rough sketch of the design anyway showing your name and the date and file this sketch away with the rest of your quilting 'stuff' – it will be interesting to compare the sketch to the photograph of the finished piece in years to come. You will notice that this presumes that you keep a photographic record of your work – if you don't already do this, please start right now!

Putting the layers together

After marking out the pattern you want to quilt comes the part everyone loves to hate – basting or tacking the three layers together so that they will not shift and move out of position while the quilting is in progress. ('In progress' is a wonderful phrase that covers a multitude of sins and can be applied to any project that has had just a few stitches put in – it sounds so much more positive than 'unfinished').

Basting or tacking is tedious but necessary unless you will be working on a traditional frame. For a small project such as a cushion or wallhanging the tedium is over fairly quickly, but full-size quilts require a certain degree of fortitude and endurance. The underlying principle of basting is that all of the layers should be smooth and wrinkle-free and be secured with sufficient lines of stitching to prevent any movement. Translated into practical terms this means that the lines have to be no more than three inches apart in any one direction. You may opt to have these lines running in either a grid (Fig 3a) or a sunburst formation

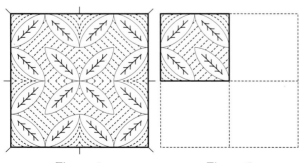

Figure 1   Figure 2

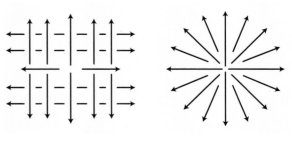

Figure 3a   Figure 3b

(Fig 3b), and the basting itself can be done with the layers on – not in – a frame, a table top or the floor – again, personal preference applies. There is a ray of hope on the basting horizon in the form of a gun which uses plastic tags to penetrate and secure the layers, with the tags then carefully snipped and removed once quilting is complete. Use of this gun drastically reduces the time it takes to baste a quilt, although it is perhaps not suitable for fragile fabrics such as fine lawn or silk.

Preparing for machine quilting requires the same closeness of basting as handquilting but instead of using stitches (which can get caught in the presser foot of the machine) it is now common practice to use quantities of small safety pins, or the gun tool just described.

Stitching tools

Needles

Needles are a vastly underrated quilting tool. We spend time deliberating over fabric and batting choices, frames, markers and virtually everything else, bar the needle we will be using. Odds are that we begin to stitch with a needle which is well past the first flush of youth even if it is of a size and type with which we are comfortable. Don't expect your needles to last forever – if you get into the habit of starting each project with a fresh needle in your hand or your sewing machine, you will enjoy the stitching rather than pulling a dulled needle through fabric or hearing bumping noises as a blunt machine needle punches its way through the layers. Needles are plentiful and relatively cheap – find a brand you like and buy several packets. If you must be economical, keep discarded needles on a separate pincushion or needlecase for such unimportant and infrequent tasks as sewing on buttons.

The usual advice when choosing needles for hand quilting is to use betweens, which are short and have a round eye. Short fine needles are easier to control during the quilting than long needles, which are more likely to bend or break as they are pushed through the three layers. You can buy betweens needles either by specific size e.g. 9s, 10s (the higher the number, the finer the needle) or by assortment e.g. 3s to 9s. If you will be hand-quilting for the first time, the assorted packet is probably the best choice as it allows you to try out the various sizes and find one that you prefer. For machine quilting use the standard needle for general sewing as specified in the handbook for your machine (now would be a good time to find the handbook) – this is likely to be a size 14/90.

Thimbles

If you never use a thimble for sewing, here is an unpalatable statement. It is very painful to quilt without a thimble somewhere on your sewing hand because you will be controlling a short fairly fine needle and pushing it through three layers. Thimbles can feel very awkward and restricting, not to mention downright peculiar, if you are not accustomed to wearing one – you are not alone in this feeling. One good way to get used to a thimble is to wear it at all times other than when you are sewing.

As with many other quilting tools and accessories there is a wide variety of thimbles to choose from – take the time to try as many different ones as you can; there is bound to be one type which feels less awkward than all the others. Your thimble needs to fit snugly without stopping the blood supply to your fingertips and you should be able to shake your hand fairly vigorously without the thimble flying off into orbit.

As you read through the description of hand quilting in Chapter Two, you will see that the fingers of the non-sewing hand come into fairly frequent contact with the point of the needle. Do you need to protect the underneath fingers in any way? Yes and no – yes if, like me, you are a devout coward and totally averse to pain; no if like most quilters you need the reassurance of feeling the point of the needle to confirm that you have gone through all the layers. If you belong to the first group, there are all manner of things you can do to protect your fingers from being shredded, ranging from thimbles to surgical tape, so be prepared to experiment. If you belong to the second group, quilt for very short periods of time and be resigned to calloused fingers.

Threads and beeswax

The best guide for choosing thread for quilting with is to use one which matches the fabric in terms of fibre content, for example cotton thread with cotton fabric, silk thread with silk and so on. Many people feel that their choice of weight of thread is restricted to those specifically marked 'quilting thread' – in fact, standard 40 or 50 count sewing thread is fine for any project which will have more than minimal quilting. The all-purpose all-polyester sewing threads are given to fraying and stretching and not always easy to work with. If you will be quilting a piece of patchwork, there is no need to keep changing the colour of the thread so that it matches the different fabrics – a medium neutral colour such as light grey or cream will work very well and 'show' far less than you might think. For large areas of one colour or for wholecloth quilting, use a colour which is at least two shades darker than the fabric for the best effect; the lines of stitching create a shadow on either side which helps create the textured effect. If the thread is an exact match, you may find that it lessens the impact of this shadow because the stitches will seem slightly paler than the surrounding fabric.

Quilting thread has a coating which not only strengthens it and reduces the likelihood of tangles and knots but helps the thread to pull through fabric easily. If you choose ordinary sewing thread, you can put a temporary coating on it by drawing the thread once or twice across a piece of beeswax and then between your thumb and index finger to remove any excess.

For machine quilting the choice of thread expands almost daily – shaded, variegated, metallic, invisible. Experiment with as many as possible to see what works well with your particular machine and what mechanical adjustments, if any, need to be made to get the best results from each one.

Frames and hoops

While it is not essential to use a hoop or frame for hand quilting, it has to be said that as a general rule, you will get a smoother crisper result if you do use one. Like so many of the other essentials for quilting there is a wide choice available and there is no single type of frame which is best for everyone. Traditionally

Quilted texture has a timeless appeal.

The lightweight nature of a tubular frame makes it relatively portable.

quilting was worked on a larger sturdier version of an embroiderer's slate or scroll frame. The frame is formed from four lengths of wood, two long, two short, which are slotted, pegged or clamped together to form a rectangle. Canvas webbing can be stapled to the two long lengths (sometimes known as rails) so that the work can be easily attached by pinning, stapling or stitching. Once attached to the rails, the tension on the work is created by the addition of the two shorter lengths of wood (or stretchers), which form the other two sides of the rectangle.

Hoops and tubular frames

Hoops and tubular frames offer today's quilter the bonus of easier access and portability for their work. Whether a hoop is better than a tubular or clip frame is largely a matter of personal preference. Both are lightweight, easy to use and adjust, and relatively inexpensive. One point to remember when using either a hoop or clip frame is that both hands should be free to concentrate on quilting. This means that you will need to arrange your quilting position so that the far edge of the hoop or frame is supported by something such as a table edge or chair arm and the near edge is supported by tucking it into your waist (or what remains of it). If this sounds far too complicated (which it isn't), you might want to consider acquiring a stand for your hoop or frame which eliminates all these physical adjustments.

Tension

Is there a correct tension to aim for when using a hoop or frame? The short answer is 'No'. All that is required is that all the layers should be smooth and free from tucks, wrinkles and other such glitches. Some quilters prefer to have the layers drumtight, others could use their work as a hammock, and most opt for a tension that is somewhere between these two extremes. Again it is a matter of experimenting to establish what works best for you.

Quilting in your hand or frameless quilting

Having said that smooth crisp quilting is generally easier to produce if a frame or hoop is used, it has to be acknowledged that there are exceptions to every rule, even general ones. A small number of quilters find that they just cannot work well with a frame or hoop and sort out their own quilting salvation without such equipment. Much to the chagrin of the more conventionally minded, these quilters can often produce work of show-winning quality, which only goes to prove that rules can be ignored – what suits you and enables you to get good results matters more than how those results are achieved. On a cautionary note it should be pointed out that whether you quilt with or without a frame, it is practice that gets results.

About the stitch

Hand quilting is easier to do than to describe. It is begun, worked and finished on the top of the quilt and is a running rather than a stab stitch. The stitches should go through all the layers and create texture on both sides of the quilt. It would be as well at this point to deal with some commonly held misconceptions about quilting stitches.

As a beginning or improving quilter please remember that the size or length of your stitches does not matter – **what you are aiming to eventually produce are stitches which appear to be even**. Small stitches are not necessarily better; evenness of stitching is your primary goal. Also, when you first try quilting, you may find yourself consumed with anxiety regarding the back – missed stitches which have not gone through all the layers and stitches of varying size. You will not improve your stitches by worrying about them and unpicking frequently. If 75 per cent of the stitches get through to the back, you are doing very well, and this percentage can only increase. There is a quilting convention which demands that top and underneath stitches should be of identical size – especially in North America. This skill is virtually impossible for most ordinary mortals to achieve irrespective of their level of expertise. So long as you are getting the majority of stitches through to the back, that is the end of the matter – all other improvements and refinements come only with practice.

Machine quilting suffers from misconceptions too. The first is that it is fiendishly difficult to do and the second that it is in some way inferior to hand quilting. Certainly, machine quilting requires practice to achieve good results, but then the same applies to hand quilting. Machine quilting is not an effortless process from which an exquisitely quilted piece emerges at the flick of a switch – it requires practice and a willingness to experiment. Anyone who has marvelled at the high standard of much of the machine quilting that is being done nowadays must agree that this technique is in no way inferior to its hand-worked counterpart – good quilting is good quilting however it has been achieved.

Bold shapes plus simple stitching equals wonderful texture. Quilt courtesy of Patricia Cox.

FINISHING TECHNIQUES

Adding borders

The simplest and fastest way to add plain borders to any project is shown in Fig 4.

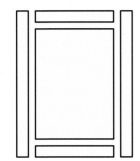

Figure 4

Measure, mark and cut strips to the width and length you require and stitch them to the main part in the sequence shown. Ideally these lengths should be seamfree but it may be that lack of fabric (or advance planning) dictates that shorter lengths need to be joined together to make the required length. If this is the case, try to arrange any seams to look intentional so that they fall at the same place on each side (Fig 5) rather than occurring at haphazard intervals around the finished border.

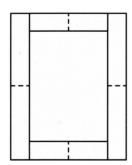

Figure 5

If you have ample border fabric, mitring the corners will add a subtle classy touch to your work (Fig 6). Avoid strongly patterned or striped fabrics the first time you try mitring. The technique itself is not difficult, but matching specific parts of a fabric pattern requires attention to detail and familiarity with the process. The simplest way I have found of achieving mitred corners is set out below and involves an absolute minimum of maths, geometry and the like.

Attach all four border strips, which must be of identical width, stopping and starting the joining

seams an exact ¼ inch (5mm) away from the corner.

You must have sufficient border fabric on all four sides to be able to overlap the strips.

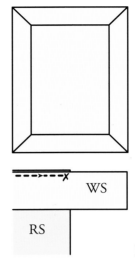

Figure 6

With the border strips in the position shown in Fig 7, carefully mark a diagonal line to connect the stop/start point to the exact place where the two strips cross (Fig 8). This will be your stitching line, so choose your marker with great care.

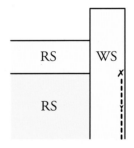

Figure 7

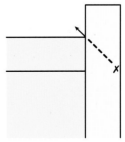

Figure 8

Fold your work so that the two border strips line up exactly and using the marked diagonal line as your guide, begin stitching at the stop/start point along to the outside edge of the strips (Fig 9). Work all four corners in the same way. Then unfold and check each corner before trimming away the surplus fabric and pressing the new seam open (Fig 10).

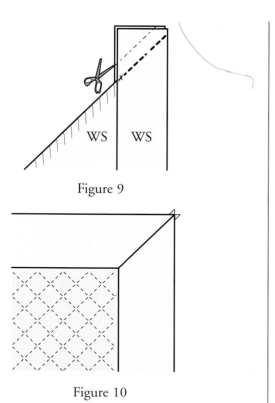

Figure 9

Figure 10

Finishing edges

There are various ways of finishing the edges of a quilt, and it is worth giving some thought as to which will be the most appropriate for each specific project, depending on whether it will receive light or heavy use. None of the techniques described here are difficult and the time taken to give each quilt the best possible finish is time well spent.

Back to front

If there is ample backing fabric remaining on all sides of the quilt, you can measure and cut it so that there is exactly the same depth of backing fabric on each side. Then trim away the top fabric and batting so that they are flush with each other and bring the backing fabric over to the front, fold under the raw edges and slip stitch into position. Then work a single line of running stitch (or alternatively machine stitch) close up against the hemmed edge of this 'binding' – this will add stability as well as improve the overall finish.

Front to back

In the same way that the backing fabric can be brought over to the front and made to look like a binding, you could take the front fabric over to the back if you wished. You will need to add the extra line of stitching in a thread to match the top fabric to help create the look of a binding.

Sides to middle

This is a finishing method frequently found on whole-cloth quilts. Both the top and backing fabrics are folded in to meet each other, and excess batting is trimmed away so that it does not extend beyond the newly folded edges, which can then be either pinned or basted into position (Fig 11). One line of running or machine stitch is worked as close to the folded edges as possible, with a second line of stitching worked a short distance away, say ¾ to 1 inch (2–2.5cm) (Fig 12).

Figure 11

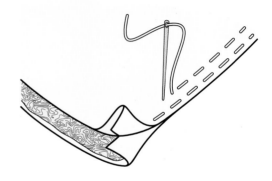

Figure 12

Binding

Single binding

This is the most economical way of finishing a quilt in terms of additional fabric. To work out how wide to cut the binding strips you need to know the width of binding you want to be visible both front and back, plus two seam allowances for hemming on each side. So if you want a 1-inch (2.5cm) binding visible both front and back, you need strips of 2 inches (5cm) plus ½ inch (1.25cm) for seams, a total of 2½ inches (6.25cm). Aim to cut the strips on the straight grain, preferably without joining. If this is not possible, join the strips so that any seams will be halfway along the finished length rather than too close to the corners. Trim all three layers of the quilt flush and put the right side of the binding in position on the right side of the quilt and line up the raw edges (Fig 13, overleaf).

Using a generous ¼ inch (5mm) seam allowance, machine stitch through all the layers. If you have a walking foot for your machine it will help keep all the layers moving evenly. Otherwise, lengthening the stitch and perhaps decreasing the tension fractionally helps you to stitch evenly. Take the binding over to the reverse of the quilt and turn under the raw edge so that the fold is touching the just-completed line of stitching (Fig 14). Slip or hem stitch the binding into place, taking care that the stitches do not go through to the right side of the quilt.

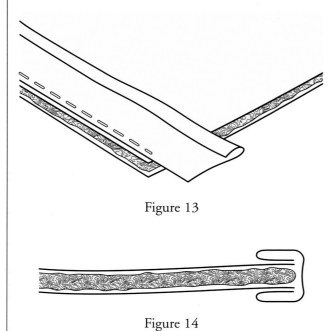

Figure 13

Figure 14

Double binding

This is a firm, hardwearing finish eminently suitable for a quilt which will have a fair degree of wear and tear. It is not economical of fabric but it gives an excellent 'handle' and finish to a quilt. However, it is perhaps not an ideal finish for miniature quilts because its relative bulk does not always translate well down to a small scale.

For quilts where the edges are supposed to finish straight, you will be best advised to cut the binding strips on the straight grain to avoid (and perhaps even restrict) any rippling or stretching of the quilt edges. For genuinely curved or scalloped-edge quilts, cut the binding strips on the bias or cross grain.

To determine the width of strip you need to cut for this type of binding, begin by deciding what depth of binding you wish to be visible on the front of the quilt. Multiply this measurement by four and add a generous ½ inch (1.25cm), then write the final figure

down. For example, say you wanted to have ½ inch (1.25cm) of binding visible on the front – four times that measurement is 2 inches (5cm) plus another ½ inch (1.25cm) for seams, which makes the width of strip required 2½ inches (6.25cm). Referring to the piece of paper which records your final figure, measure, mark and cut sufficient strips of this width from the binding fabric. Fold each strip in half with wrong sides together and cut edges matching, and press carefully. Trim away any excess batting and backing from the quilt edges so that the edges are flush and also as straight as possible. Pin the first strip into position on the top of the quilt with all cut edges aligned.

Stitch, by hand or machine, through all the layers, maintaining a consistent seam allowance of ¼ inch (5mm) (Fig 15). If you have a walking foot for your machine, this would be a good time to use it as it will help keep all the layers moving evenly.

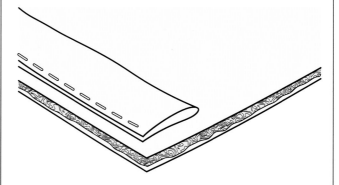

Figure 15

After attaching all the binding strips to the quilt, fold the binding over to the reverse side so that the folded edge just covers the line of stitching and hem the binding in place by hand using a matching thread.

Corners

Quilts have an irritating habit of having more than one corner, and corners require that you think about how to put the binding around them so that you have square, well-bound corners to your quilt. Butted corners are simple to do and are appropriate for both single- and double-fold bindings. The binding strips are overlapped (Fig 16) and the raw edges are then turned under before being stitched into place (Figs 17 and 18).

Mitred corners take more words and diagrams to explain, but are actually just as straightforward to make. Join the folded and pressed binding strips into one continuous length, which must measure the same as the perimeter of the quilt plus a generous add-on

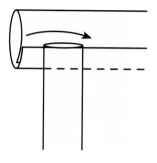

Figure 16

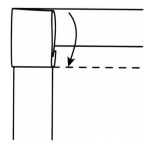

Figure 17

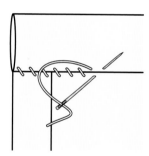

Figure 18

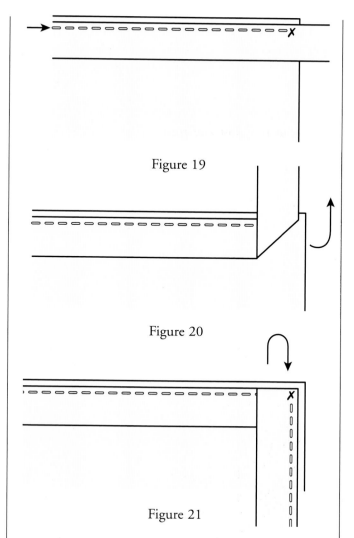

Figure 19

Figure 20

Figure 21

allowance for the corners of 6 to 12 inches (15 to 30cm). Always overestimate required lengths for bindings of any sort. There is nothing so frustrating as finding that the strip has run out just a few inches (or centimetres) short. Starting from the midpoint of one side, position and pin the binding so that the cut edges are flush with the quilt's trimmed edge. When you reach the first corner put a pin at the exact spot where the two seam allowances will meet (Fig 19).

Now fold the strip up through 45 degrees (Fig 20) and pin along this diagonal fold. Bring the unattached strip length back over to cover this diagonal fold. The top fold should line up with the edge of the binding.

Machine stitch the first length of binding into place, stopping on the spot when you reach the corner. Fold to make the mitre before continuing on to the second section (Fig 21).

If you stitch, mitre, check and then stitch some more, it is easier to correct any errors than if you stitch everything in place before checking that the mitres are how you would like them to be. Once all the binding is stitched and folded into position, turn the folded edge over to the back of the quilt ready to be hemmed into place. The corners on both front and back of the quilt should fold into neat mitres. With a little practice this whole process is much simpler to do than it is to describe.

Piping

Piping or cording on the edges of a cushion, quilt or wallhanging gives a subtle and sophisticated finish and is not difficult to do. Choose a thickness of polyester piping cord appropriate to your project (cotton cord requires pre-shrinking) and cut bias fabric strips wide enough to enclose the cord and leave at least ½ inch (1.25cm) seam allowance. Fold the bias strip over the cord right side out and stitch as close as you can to the cord (Fig 22, overleaf). Use a thread that tones with the fabric and a zipper foot on the machine. Pin the length of covered piping in position on top of the quilt with the raw edges flush to the quilt edges and stitch the piping to the quilt top (Fig 23) only. Trim away any excess batting and quilt top, fold the backing fabric over so that all the raw edges are enclosed, and slip or hem stitch the backing to finish (Fig 24).

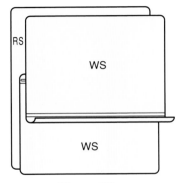

Figure 25

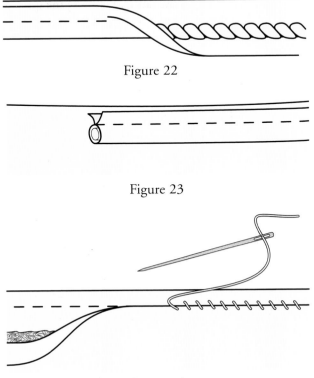

Figure 22

Figure 23

Figure 24

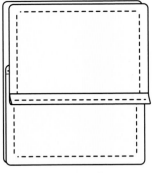

Figure 26

Making cushions

There are various ways of making up cushions, some more intricate and time-consuming than others. I can strongly recommend being fortunate enough to have a mother who is an expert at zippers and piping and willing to put these talents to use at great speed and very short notice. If you lack this unfair advantage, the simplest way to turn your work into a cushion is the 'envelope' method. For this you will need to make two rectangles, each about three-quarters as large as your cushion front, from your backing fabric and machine hem each one along one long edge. Then lay both rectangles with the hemmed edges overlapping and right sides facing the right side of the cushion front (Fig 25). Pin along all the edges and machine stitch around the complete shape (Fig 26).

Trim away excess fabric to leave seams of ⅜ inch (1cm) or ½ inch (1.25cm), making an angled cut across each of the four corners. Turn the work right side out through the hemmed slit at the back.

Pressing

Like basting, pressing is a necessary evil and should not be skimped in your rush to get on to the quilting. Marking and quilting are much easier if the fabrics are well-pressed and wrinkle-free, piecing accuracy can be improved with good pressing at each stage of construction, and so on – just try not to let anyone see you doing this in case they mistakenly think that you might apply these principles to ordinary household laundry. 'Steam or dry' is a momentous decision for you to make and there are any number of strong opinions on this. My advice is to go with whatever feels right to you, but remember that pressing for piecing means pressing – i.e., no enthusiastic moving of the iron from side to side.

Laundering

The majority of projects in this book were designed with practical everyday use in mind. As a general rule, if you have used cotton fabrics and either cotton or polyester batting for your quilting, there is no reason why the finished piece should not be washed, unless of course you have used a mixture of dark, bright and pale colours which you neglected to pre-wash or test for colourfastness before you began. Once you have washed a quilted item, it will never again look quite as crisp as it did when you took the last stitch. But once household dirt and fair wear and tear take their toll it will need to be washed or cleaned. Washing is best done using lukewarm water and a gentle cleaning agent rather than one of the standard family wash detergents. Minimum handling, agitation and brief spin drying are the other requirements, followed by drying flat, preferably in the open air. If you have used cotton batting, you may find that a short turn in a tumble dryer will take some of the stronger creases out. If you are lucky enough to own an old or antique quilt, take expert advice before trying to clean it. It may be possible to launder it or have it professionally dry-cleaned, but check first.

Labelling

In an ideal world all the quilts ever made would be labelled with the name and address of the maker and the name of the recipient, the year it was made, and a host of other deeply significant details. If this were the case, quilt historians past, present and future would have a much easier job in identifying and dating quilts. **Please** put a simple label on everything you make, masterpiece or mistake; there is no knowing where various pieces of your work will be in another fifty years' time and a label will add to someone else's enjoyment and information. All you need to make a label is a small piece of light-coloured plain fabric and a waterproof pen with a fine point. Write the information on the fabric and hem it in position somewhere on the reverse of the quilt. Technology enthusiasts who have a computer and printer available can design their labels onscreen and then print them directly onto fabric which has been temporarily stiffened by ironing it onto freezer paper.

Hanging sleeves

If you intend to hang a quilt as a decorative furnishing, take a careful look at the intended position – is it exposed to direct sunlight? Sunlight has a powerful fading effect on fabrics over even a short period of time, and also weakens the fabric. Hanging the quilt is best done by adding a sleeve to the reverse side so that a rod can be slipped through to support the weight evenly. Thumbtacks (drawing pins) pushed straight through the quilt layers into the wall are a definite no. A hanging sleeve is easily made by cutting a 6-inch (15cm) wide strip of fabric which is just a little shorter than the upper edge of the quilt, folding it in half, right sides facing, and stitching along the long edge to make a tube (Fig 27). Turn the tube right side out and hem the edges at both ends. Then press with the seam in the middle of one side before pinning and stitching the sleeve into position on the back of the quilt (Fig 28). Make sure your stitches do not go through to the front of the quilt.

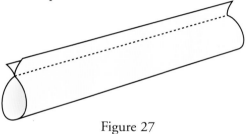

Figure 27

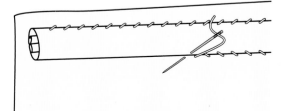

Figure 28

CHAPTER TWO

Traditional Wholecloth Quilting

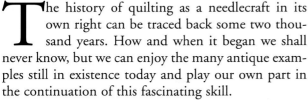

The history of quilting as a needlecraft in its own right can be traced back some two thousand years. How and when it began we shall never know, but we can enjoy the many antique examples still in existence today and play our own part in the continuation of this fascinating skill.

The most frequently used definition of quilting is that it is a textile sandwich – how it was defined before the sandwich was invented remains a mystery. There are traditionally three layers in quilting: a top fabric, batting and a backing fabric. Stitching these three layers together not only secures them but also produces a decorative texture.

Talking about quilting in general descriptive terms can make it seem an academic and rather unapproachable needlecraft. Despite its long and illustrious history it is worth reminding ourselves that not only is it a simple craft which anyone can do but also that it has a wide scope, ranging from the purely decorative to functional working domestic textiles. Roughly translated, you can make a quilted wallhanging for all to admire or you can make cushions and quilts to use on an everyday basis.

Tools and equipment

Like many other traditional needlecrafts quilting requires only the most basic of tools and equipment. This does not prevent most quilters from gradually acquiring a positive battery of gadgets, tools and general supplies, but the essential items needed to begin quilting are easily obtained and not too expensive (see Chapter One).

Fabric choice and colour are important considerations for wholecloth quilting since the texture created by the design is paramount and there are no distractions of other colours and shapes. We all have our own favourite colours and you will not go far wrong if you are guided by your own preferences. The type of fabric can be as plain or fancy as you choose, ranging from silk or satin to humble dressweight cotton. One of the fascinating aspects of quilting is the way it can change the appearance of a fabric so a plain cotton fabric which has been heavily or extensively quilted can take on a subtle richness and suggestion of sheen. 'Fancy' fabrics such as satin or silk are good subjects for quilting but require a little care in handling and marking and are perhaps more appropriate choices for quilters with some experience. Certainly for your first few wholecloth quilting projects, a standard dressweight cotton fabric is ideal.

Types of patterns

You can quilt virtually any type of pattern and get a pleasing textured result. As a general rule open flowing line patterns usually work better than those with tightly packed angular lines. To put it another way, stylised patterns are preferable to more realistic ones, as the spaces between the lines of stitching rather than the stitching itself are the elements that define the pattern to the eye. If you look at old quilts, you will often see the same pattern idea being used in slightly varying ways over and over again. This is undoubtedly due as much to quilters finding patterns which worked and using them repeatedly, as to liking a pattern for its own sake or having limited imagination.

Sources of patterns

So you want to try quilting. Where do you find patterns? The projects in this book should provide enough ideas to get you started, and there are any number of quilting patterns and stencils, books and magazines to offer you further inspiration. To begin with the best advice is to keep your pattern choices simple and be prepared to experiment. You will soon

Cushions are ideal quilting projects, being small enough to complete quickly and of a manageable size.

develop a sense of what you like and what works well for you. You could even try creating patterns yourself. See page 122 for information on cutting paper shapes.

Elements of design

While it is the unquilted space – the spaces between the lines of quilting – that define the pattern itself, much of the success of a quilted design lies in balance, simplicity and contrast. As you will see in many of the projects that follow, the curved lines of the main pattern motifs are enhanced by the use of contrasting straight lines to fill in some or all of the background spaces.

The quilting stitch

The running stitch used for hand quilting is begun, worked and finished on the top of the work. It is not a stab stitch, which can be slow to work and often gives an uneven line on the reverse side, nor is it begun and finished on the back. You can execute the running stitch in any way that feels comfortable to you and produces an acceptable result – there is no one way which is absolutely correct. The following description of the mechanics of quilting may be helpful to you so long as you remember that you will need some practice before you reach the stage where the process requires only minimum effort and concentration.

Begin by threading a betweens needle with an 18 to 20-inch (45 to 50cm) length of thread of your choice. You do not have to measure this length exactly, it is just a guide. Make a knot about 1 inch (2.5cm) from the freshly cut end. Decide where you want to begin stitching and slide the point of the needle into the top fabric, along the batting and back out through the top fabric roughly 1 inch (2.5cm) away from your planned starting point (Fig 1). Pull the length of the thread through until the knot engages with the top fabric and prevents you from pulling it further. Now is the time for a short firm tug on the thread, the knot should make a satisfying 'popping' noise and disappear through the top fabric, where it will lie out of sight and anchored in the batting (Fig 2). If you are

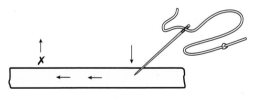

Figure 1

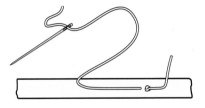

Figure 2

over-zealous with this short firm tug, you may find that you have pulled the knot completely through the layers. In this case try again with a little less muscle. Your first stitch can be a back stitch through the top two, or all three layers of the quilt, or you could begin with a single stitch – again, it is a question of what feels 'right' for you. And here we come to the crunch – how do you make running stitches through three layers which may be held in a hoop or frame? Spread the fingers of your non-sewing hand underneath your work so that one of the fingers pushes upwards and makes a slight bump on the top surface. This not only compresses the layers slightly but gives you a target at which to aim the needle's point. Put the needle in as near to vertical as possible (Fig 3).

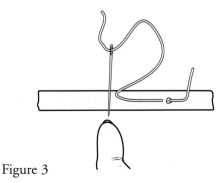

Figure 3

The next step is to lay the needle down so that it is virtually horizontal, or parallel to the fabric (Fig 4) and push it so that the point emerges on the top of the work a short distance away from the point of entry (Fig 5, opposite). This sounds horribly complicated

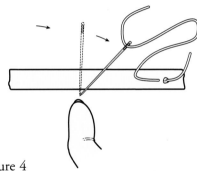

Figure 4

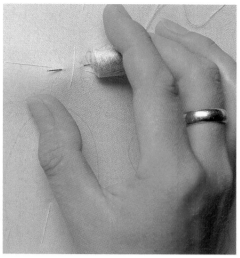

When starting to quilt, bring the needle out on the marked stitching line.

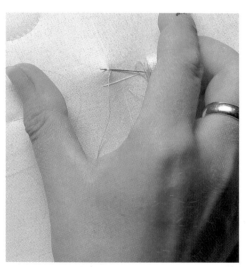

Taking a single stitch.

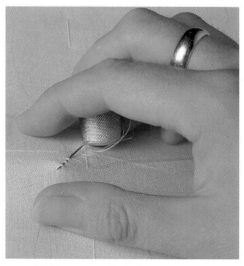

Taking several stitches at a time.

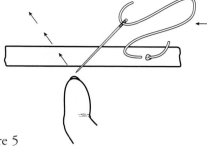

Figure 5

and impossible because it is a written description rather than a slow moving picture. Look again at the diagrams and put your sewing hand into the positions shown. What happens is that as the needle goes down through the layers, your hand is parallel to the fabric – needle vertical, hand horizontal. To bring the needle back out again, you move it from vertical to horizontal: needle horizontal, hand vertical. Your wrist has moved your hand through ninety degrees – clockwise if you are right-handed, anti-clockwise if you are left-handed. This is the basis of the small rocking movement which characterises hand quilting. The need for a thimble on your sewing hand becomes apparent when you try to push the needle through the quilt layers to complete the stitch (or stitches). Whether you make single stitches or load two or more stitches onto the needle really doesn't matter. You are aiming eventually to achieve stitches which appear to be even.

It is not necessary to pull the full length of thread through the layers for each stitch or group of stitches. Try pulling just a little through each time so that the length of thread is gradually taken up. Then pull it completely through after a good number of stitches have been made.

Moving from one line to another without finishing off and re-starting is easily done. After making the last stitch bring the needle back to the top of the work a short distance away and gently pull the remaining length of thread through to the top also. Put the point of the needle onto the thread where it emerges through the top layer (Fig 6) and then slide the needle down through the top layer alongside the thread, along the batting and bring it up at the point where

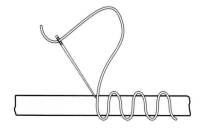

Figure 6

you want to begin stitching (Fig 7). Putting the point of the needle on the emerging thread will cause a small split stitch to form as the thread is taken through the top two layers, giving it extra anchorage as it lies in the batting.

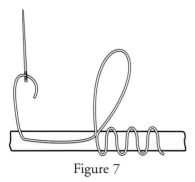

Figure 7

Sometimes you may need to move from one line of stitching to another. Try 'travelling' the needle in the following way – another instruction that is easier to do than to explain.

Put the needle, point first, through the top fabric and into the batting. Push the needle away as far as you can through the batting before bringing the point of the needle out to the top of the work. Leave the eye of the needle in the batting and push the needle tip so that you can swivel the needle on its eye. Guide the needle, eye first, through the batting again and push it out, still eye first, to the top of the work ready to begin stitching again. With this swivelling/pivoting action, alternating the point and the eye of the needle, you can move around under the top fabric without making any telltale marks or stitches. You can follow the point/eye sequence more than once to travel further, but for such distances or to move more than say 3 inches (7.5cm), it may be more secure to finish off and start a fresh thread.

Finishing off is basically the reverse of the starting process. Make the last stitch and bring needle and thread to the top. Make a knot in the thread about ½ inch (1.25cm) away from the top and then put the needle back through the top (Fig 8), run it along the batting

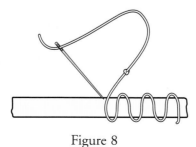

Figure 8

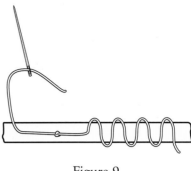

Figure 9

and finally out to the top again, 'popping' the knot through the top layer exactly as for starting (Fig 9).

Both the starting and finishing ends of thread can then be clipped away. Make sure you keep the scissor blades parallel to the top rather than dipping towards it, which invites inadvertent cutting of the top fabric.

More than one way to quilt

The quilting stitch described above is based on running stitch worked from side to side across the body, or laterally if you want to sound really grand. Working on a free-standing traditional quilting frame shows up the limitations of this technique. From time to time you will be stitching in an uncomfortable direction or needing to work strongly curved lines in two parts. Quilting with a hoop or tubular frame allows you to keep turning the work so that you are always working in a comfortable direction. Being self-taught meant that, having found a way of quilting which worked for me and which many other quilters were also using, it was some years before I had the opportunity to try any other method, but here is a brief description of the thumb quilting technique which I do recommend. Instead of working across from side to side, you will be working away from yourself using your thumb to control the top of the needle (Fig 10). You will certainly

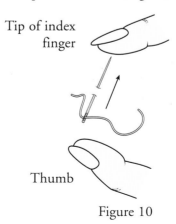

Tip of index finger

Thumb

Figure 10

need to find some sort of protection for your thumb – a tailors' thimble, leather thimble, etc., so that the movement of the needle is between the thumb and index finger rather than the middle finger and thumb. One of the benefits of mastering this quilting technique is that it greatly reduces the stress on the wrist of your sewing hand and makes good use of the strength of your thumb for pushing and controlling the needle. You may also wish to try quilting towards yourself (using your middle finger to control the needle – Fig 11) rather than from side to side to see if that

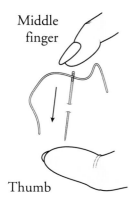

Middle finger

Thumb

Figure 11

is a more comfortable direction in which to sew. In other words, there is more than one way of controlling the needle when you are quilting and there is no 'right' or 'wrong' – whatever feels right for you and helps you to get a good result (remember, even, not small, stitches plus practice) is the best.

Stitch size

When you first begin to quilt (and for some time after that), your stitches will not be wonderful either in terms of size or evenness. Practice **will** make a difference. So many quilters are dismissive of their work saying 'Of course my stitches are far too large' – too large for what? The function of the running stitch used in quilting is to secure the layers and produce texture; even stitches (whatever their size) give a clearly defined line for the eye to follow. Pursuing the Holy Grail of tiny stitches does not always make for even stitches and can drastically reduce the pleasure that should be inherent in quilting. Everyone has a stitch size which is natural to them, be it large or small, and unless you are terrified of the mythical Quilting

Police, there is little point in putting major effort into reducing the size of your stitches when you should be enjoying quilting and allowing yourself to improve at a comfortable pace and relaxed pace. Take a few steps back from your work – look at the pattern and texture and notice how insignificant those 'inferior' stitches have become in the overall scheme of things. Remember the well-worn maxim of 'Don't run before you can walk'.

The reverse side

The temptation when quilting to want to constantly turn the work over and examine the back can be almost unbearable. This scrutiny nearly always results in the unpicking of some of the stitches because they were judged 'not quite right' or you felt you could do better. If you continue to quilt a little, look a little and unpick a little, you will soon be very skilled at unpicking (or reverse quilting if you want to sound positive), but your quilting will not have improved one jot. Confidence and some semblance of stitching rhythm will make improvements that constant checking does not permit, so if you are new to quilting, ignore what is happening on the reverse side for as long as possible and just concentrate on the top. When you do finally crack under the strain and inspect the back, here is a percentage guideline: 50 per cent stitches actually visible on the reverse is good, 75 per cent is marvellous and anything higher is stratospheric. Keep telling yourself that you will improve and don't look at the back too often.

A persistent rumble of complaint which is often heard from new and improving quilters runs like this: 'My stitches are smaller on the back than they are on the front – what am I doing wrong?' or 'Why can't I get the stitches to look the same front and back?' Allow me to express a strongly felt conviction; quilting is enjoyable and the final result has a delightful texture. The more you quilt, the better you quilt. Unless your goal is to win a fistful of blue ribbons for your quilting in competitive shows with your very first piece of quilting, it is more positive and productive to quilt with an uncritical attitude. Yes, your stitches may be smaller on the back, but is this an imprisonable offence? Are you terrified of a dawn raid from the Stitch Police? The only 'trick' which will make all your stitches even, front or back, is to allow yourself time and practice.

SIX CUSHIONS

Cushions are an ideal size for a first quilting project, small enough to complete quickly and of a manageable size. If, like many quilters, you eventually find yourself surrounded by a multitude of cushions, remember that they make impressive gifts to non-quilting friends! The cushions shown on page 23 would be ideal practice pieces for a beginning quilter. By the way, the definition of a beginning quilter is one who has yet to make the first cushion. After just one cushion, there is immediate promotion to the heady status of improving quilter!

YOU WILL NEED

Aqua Arabesque Cushion
20-inch (50cm) square of fabric for top

Spiral Fan Cushion
20-inch (50cm) square of fabric for top

Chris's Special Cushion
24-inch (60cm) square of fabric for top

Celtic Star Cushion
20-inch (50cm) square of fabric for top

Feather Square Cushion
20-inch (50cm) square of fabric for top

Cream Curls Cushion
16-inch (40cm) square of fabric for top

A square of lightweight 2-ounce batting at least 2 inches (5cm) larger than the top fabric
A square of fabric for the backing which is the same measurement as the batting
Fabric for the back of the cushion – this also should be 2 inches (5cm) larger than the top fabric to allow for seams (see also envelope method, page 20)

FOR ALL CUSHIONS YOU WILL ALSO NEED

Fabric marker
Basting (tacking) thread
Quilting thread (see page 12 for information on choosing thread)
Betweens needle of your choice for quilting
Quilting hoop or frame
Tracing or greaseproof paper and black felt marker

1　Choose one of the quarter patterns that follow and trace onto tracing or greaseproof paper. Use this to mark out the complete design onto paper.

2　Press both top and backing fabrics to remove any creases and wrinkles.

3　If you have chosen a light-coloured fabric, you will be able to mark the design on the fabric by tracing it through with a marker of your choice (see page 9). If you are using a dark fabric, you will need to use a light box or similar arrangement and a light-coloured marker (see page 10). Whichever method you use, remember to mark lightly and also to check that you have copied all the lines of the design onto the fabric before lifting it away from the tracing. If you have chosen one of the designs which features crosshatching at the centre, it is not necessary to mark in all the lines at this stage. You may prefer to wait until you have quilted the main design and then decide a) if you want to do any more quilting, and b) what scale and type of crosshatching you think would look best. Perhaps double lines, or double lines going diagonally in just one direction – the choice is yours, and you can use short lengths of masking tape (see pages 10–11) to mark the arrangement of lines you decide on.

When the design is marked on the top fabric, assemble and baste the three layers of the quilt sandwich together (see page 11), then you are ready to begin quilting.

4　Take a few moments to review the information on quilting on pages 14–15. Decide whether you will begin at the centre or in one corner of the design. Then thread the needle and start to quilt. If you are quilting for the first time, please resist the temptation to be over-critical of yourself. Of course, your stitches will not be as even as those of an 'old hand' but they will improve, particularly if you relax and just enjoy the texture that quilting creates.

5　When all the design has been quilted, make up your cushion by your favourite method.

With one cushion successfully completed, why not put your experience to good use and make one of the other designs?

The Spiral Fan Cushion is 15 inches (38cm) square.

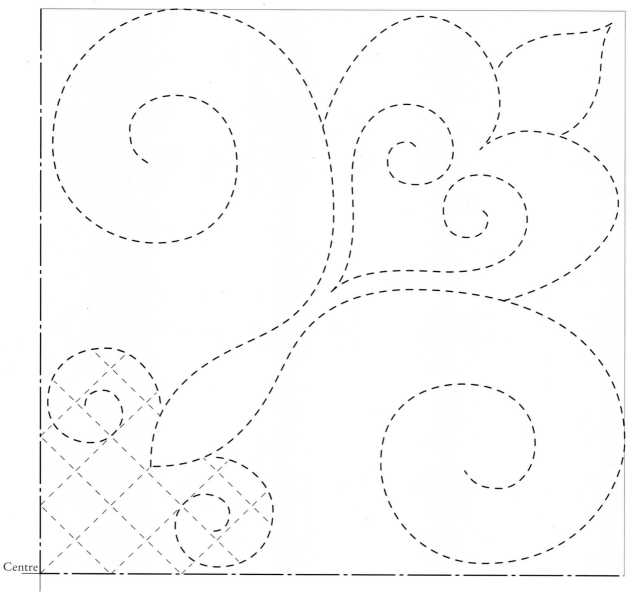

Centre

SPIRAL FAN CUSHION FULL SIZE PATTERN

The Aqua Arabesque Cushion is 15 inches (38cm) square.

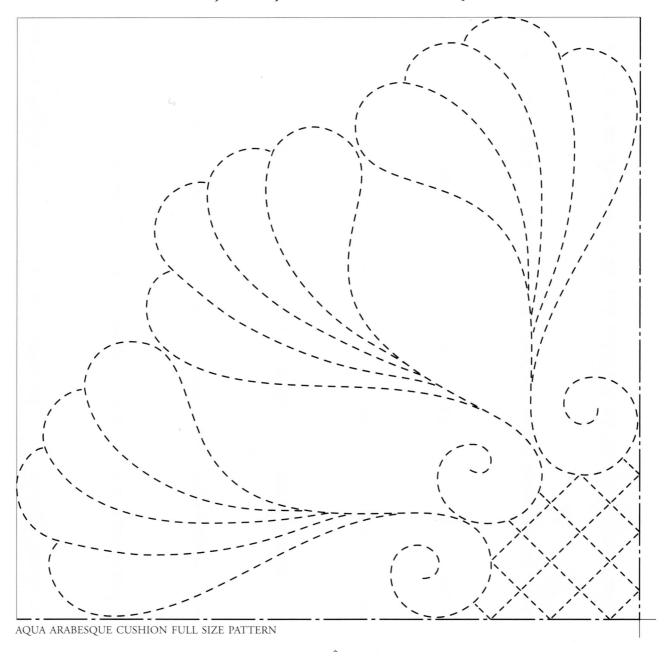

AQUA ARABESQUE CUSHION FULL SIZE PATTERN

Chris's Special Cushion is 19 inches (48cm) square.

Centre

CHRIS'S SPECIAL CUSHION PATTERN – enlarge by 142%

The Celtic Star Cushion is 15 inches (38cm) square.

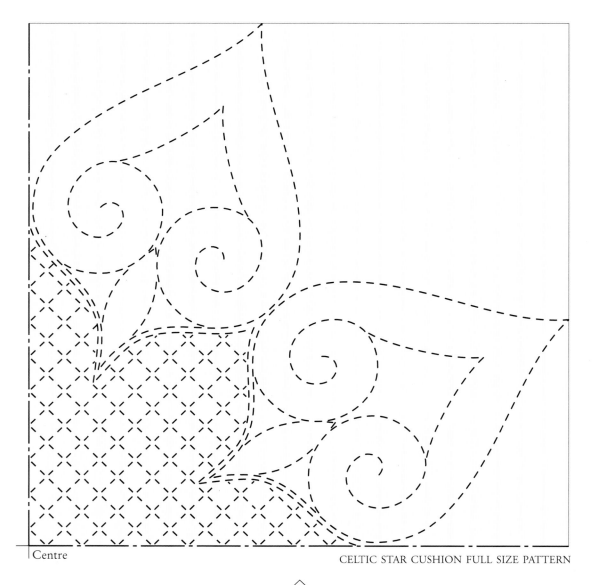

Centre

CELTIC STAR CUSHION FULL SIZE PATTERN

The Feather Square Cushion is 15 inches (38cm) square.

Centre

FEATHER SQUARE CUSHION FULL SIZE PATTERN

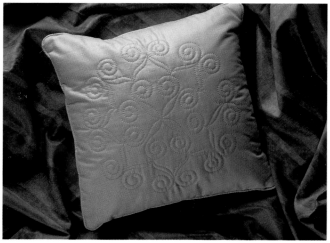

The Cream Curls Cushion is 15 inches (38cm) square.

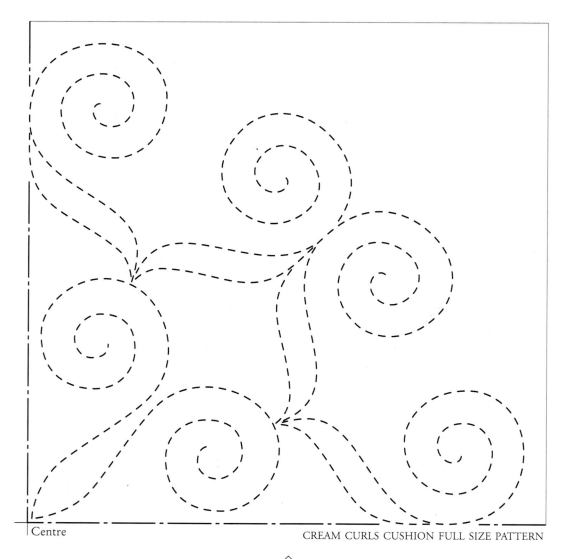

Centre

CREAM CURLS CUSHION FULL SIZE PATTERN

SIMPLE STRIPPY

The inspiration for this project was a well-worn wholecloth quilt. Strippy quilts are reassuringly simple to make; the piecing is minimal and the patterns are of a comfortably large scale which makes for easy marking and quilting. Whatever your level of quilting experience you should have fun (and lots of quilting practice) making this quilt.

YOU WILL NEED

2 yards (2m) of two contrasting or toning fabrics for strips
4 yards (4m) of fabric for backing
Lightweight batting – pre-cut single-bed size pack
Thread, quilting needles, thimble
Hoop or frame
Fabric marker
Template material and tracing paper

Finished size: 56 x 72 inches (142 x 182cm)

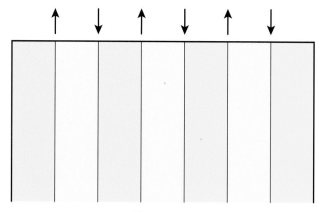

Figure 12

1   Make templates from the patterns on pages 38–40, or trace the patterns and use them to make a complete Master Sheet if your fabric choices mean you can use the trace-through marking method (page 10).

2   Pre-wash and press your fabrics before measuring and cutting the strips. Strippy quilts traditionally have an 'odd' number of strips (5, 7, 9, etc.) but there is no rule about the arrangement of dark and light strips. So for this quilt, which has a total of 7 strips, you could have 4 dark and 3 light strips with dark strips at each side, or you could have 4 light and 3 dark strips with the light strips falling at each side. Whichever arrangement you decide on, you will need to cut strips 10 inches (25cm) wide, which allows for standard ¼-inch (5mm) seams.

3   Join the strips together, taking seams of ¼ inch (5mm) and reversing the stitching direction of the seams as shown in Fig 12, above. This helps to keep

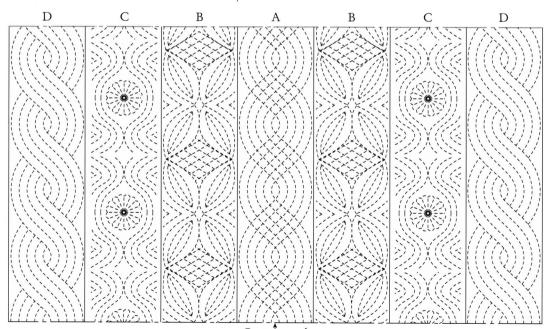

Figure 13

D   C   B   A   B   C   D

Centre panel

everything as straight as possible, without undue rippling or bowing out of true.

4 When all the strips have been joined together, press the seams either to the dark side or open as you prefer. I usually press seams open so there is a more even distribution of seam allowance on either side, rather than stitch through three layers on one side of the seam.

5 Measure and then lightly mark the centre of each strip. This will help you to keep the pattern aligned as you mark it onto the fabric, whether you use templates or trace it through as described on page 10.

Using your chosen marker and marking method you can now put the pattern onto the fabric (Fig 13, page 35, shows suggestions). Work systematically one strip at a time. It may be helpful if you begin at the centre of each strip and work out to the edges.

6 Join fabric widths to make the backing to the required size. Press the seam(s) open and then press the completed backing.

7 Spread out the three layers – backing (wrong side up), batting and strippy top (right side up) – and baste them together.

8 Quilt! You might choose to begin at one edge of an outer strip and work along to the opposite edge, quilting one strip at a time and moving in the same direction on each strip, which is how traditional strippies were worked on a large floor frame.

9 When the quilting is complete, finish or neaten the edges. The usual choice for the traditional style of this strippy quilt would be a 'sides to middle' finish (see page 17), although you could bind the edges in a toning or matching fabric if you prefer.

10 Please remember to make a label for your new creation. Do make it now rather than promising yourself you will get 'around to it' later.

This lovely blue strippy is a reproduction of an antique quilt, quilted with care by Ann Jermey.

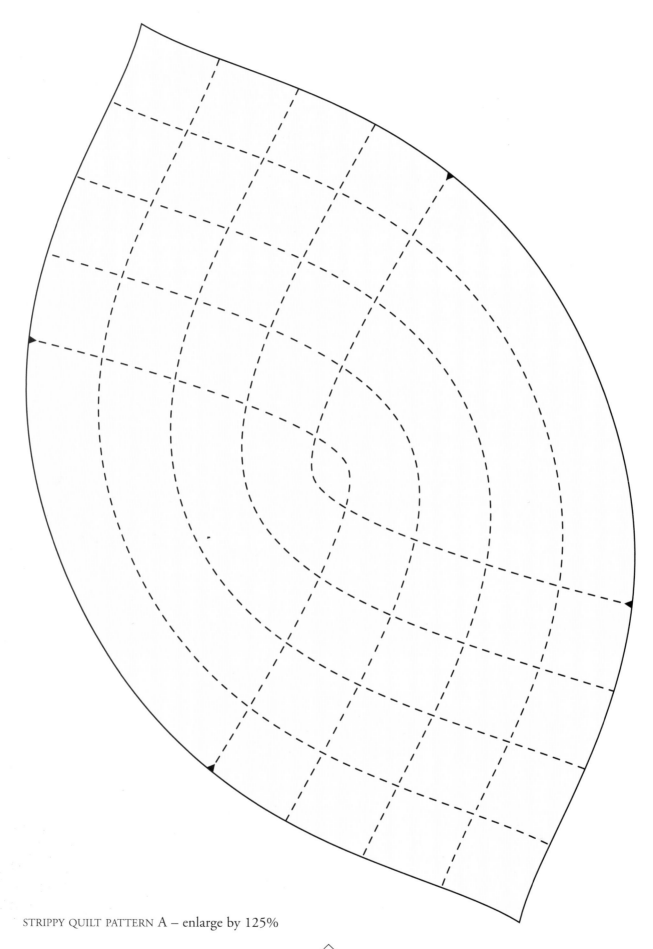

STRIPPY QUILT PATTERN A – enlarge by 125%

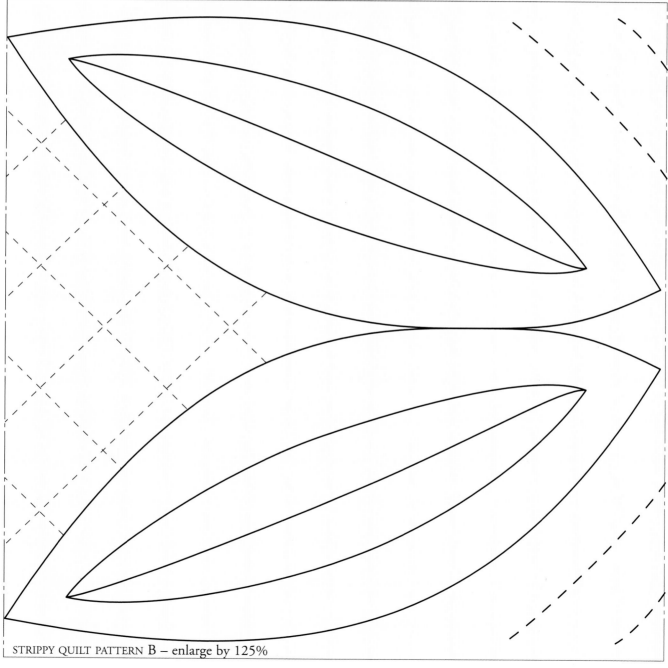

STRIPPY QUILT PATTERN B – enlarge by 125%

STRIPPY QUILT PATTERN C – enlarge by 125%

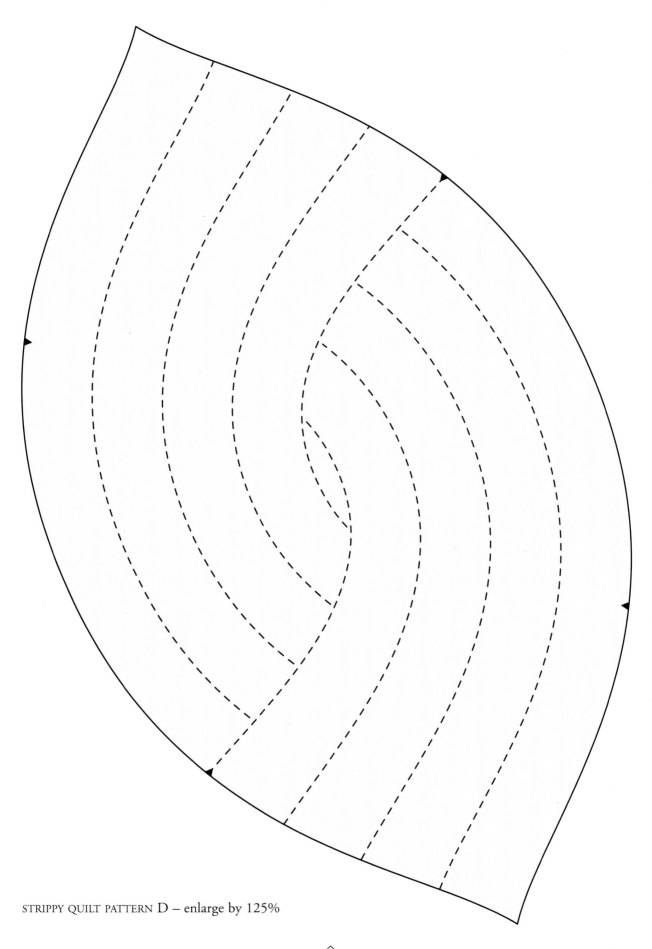

STRIPPY QUILT PATTERN D – enlarge by 125%

SANDIE'S BLUE QUILT

This prize-winning crib quilt made by Sandie Lush should not be the first quilting project you undertake, but it is not as difficult as it may seem at first glance. The overall impression of complexity is derived from the scale of the rich feathered design and the excellent contrast between the main design and the background quilting, all beautifully stitched on satin fabric.

YOU WILL NEED

1½ yards (1.5m) of top fabric
1½ yards (1.5m) of backing fabric
36 x 50-inch (92 x 127cm) piece of lightweight
(2-ounce) batting
Quilting needle
Thread of your choice to tone with the top fabric
Hoop or frame
Fabric marker
Template material and tracing paper
Medium black marker pen
A little patience

Finished size: 42 x 30 inches (107 x 76cm)

1 Press all the fabrics.
2 Trace the patterns on pages 44–45 onto a full-size Master Sheet (see page 11) to make the complete design. Go over your pencil lines with a medium black marker pen for greater clarity.
3 Tape the Master Sheet onto a smooth surface and slip some white paper underneath the master to make the lines easier to see. Tape the top fabric in position over the Master Sheet and carefully trace the design through using a fabric marker of your choice.

Of course, you will not need to be reminded to select a marker carefully and to check the marking for visibility and ease of removal. (Sandie used water-soluble crayon and a water-soluble pen.)

Double-check that you have traced all sections of the design before lifting off the fabric.
4 Spread out the three layers and baste them together (see page 11), taking great care to keep them smooth and wrinkle-free before and during the basting process.
5 Work the quilting. When you quilt lightweight or 'awkward' fabrics such as satin or silk, take extra care with handling if you are using a frame or hoop. Do not leave the work in the hoop except when you are actually stitching and be scrupulously systematic with regard to the quilting sequence. For this particular design you could begin either at one corner or in the centre. Sandie chose to quilt all the feathers first and then marked and quilted the background patterns. Being a conscientious quilter, she also kept the quilt in an old pillowcase between stitching sessions, which helped to keep the work clean.
6 The 'sides to middle' method of neatening and finishing quilt edges (page 17) is perhaps less appropriate for this project than piping (page 19) or binding (page 17) the edges, although, as always, this is a personal choice.
7 At the risk of being repetitive, please remember to make and attach a label to the finished quilt.

Sandie chose to stitch the feather designs (above) first when she made her quilt, but you could start at one corner or in the centre. The finished quilt (opposite) shows the perfect results which can be achieved with delicate satin.

Centre

SANDIE'S BLUE QUILT PATTERN – enlarge by 158%

DI'S WHITE QUILT

You may be wondering why a second small quilt which seems to belong in the 'I could never...' category has been selected as a project. The reason is that, like the preceding project, this quilt is of a highly manageable size and also happens to be a shining example of how close quilting can transform a plain white cotton fabric. Furthermore, it gives you a wonderful opportunity to practise and refine your quilting without having to wrestle with large quantities of fabric, batting and backing. While stitching this quilt, its maker, Diane Clarke, became totally hooked on closely spaced quilting (as you can see from the border detail) and has since succumbed to the delights of stipple quilting (see pages 54 and 55). And, of course, there are always exceptions to rules. Having stated earlier that quilting is a running stitch, not a stab stitch, it is immensely painful to have to relate that all the stitching on this piece was achieved by the stabbing method!

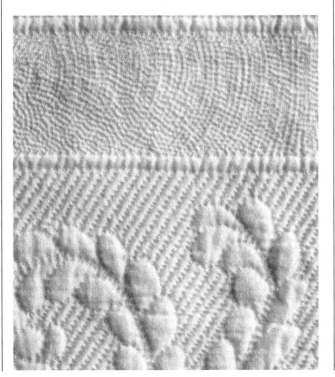

¾ yard (0.75m) of top fabric
¾ yard (0.75m) of backing fabric
26 x 36-inch (66 x 91cm) piece of lightweight (2-ounce) batting
Basting thread
Quilting thread
Needles
Fabric marker
Template material – Tracing paper and pencil
Medium black marker pen
Good eyesight, reading glasses and patience

Finished size: 32 x 22 inches (81 x 55cm)

1 Prewash and press all fabrics.
2 Trace the quarter pattern from pages 48–49 onto a Master Sheet and complete the design, then go over the pencil lines with a black marker.

Use the trace-through method (see page 10) to transfer the complete design to the top fabric with the marker you have chosen. Remember to take the time to test your marker first – Diane used very light pencil.
3 Next, baste the three layers together closely (see page 11) – take care in choosing the colour of basting thread if you are using a pale or white fabric.
4 Take several deep breaths and start stitching. Working out from the centre will probably be best for this project, with closely quilted areas stitched after the main design has been completed. If you are confident about your choices of background quilting style and scale, you can, of course, work these areas as you come to them rather than returning to fill them in.

It is perhaps an understatement to request that you allow yourself the luxury of time for the quilting of this project. It may be small in size, but this is not something to be done in a rush. It should be savoured and enjoyed. Working to a short deadline on a complex closely quilted item is not a good idea and only leads to frayed temper.
5 The original quilt is finished with fine piping; an alternative would be to use a very narrow binding.
6 It is imperative that an heirloom piece such as this has a label!

Diane Clarke's exquisitely stitched white on white crib quilt shows just how effective quilting can be.

Centre

CHAPTER THREE

Trapunto and Corded Quilting

Whether traditional layered quilting is an older technique than trapunto quilting is an academic question best left to the academics – both have an impressively long history and there are many examples of the two being used together. Trapunto is the generic term for quilted shapes and lines which have been corded or stuffed, although nowadays we usually refer to cording and trapunto as being distinct types of quilting.

CORDED OR ITALIAN QUILTING

For a technique which is often associated with 'fancy work', corded quilting is remarkably straightforward and quick to do, and it is somewhat surprising that, despite a short revival in the early 1950s, it is not as popular as it deserves to be. Perhaps the renewed interest in its companion technique, trapunto or stuffed quilting (see page 53) will help to bring this rather neglected branch of quilting back into the limelight.

Corded quilting has a special appeal all of its own and also has the added attraction of being a relatively fast technique to work. I readily admit to being prejudiced in favour of this type of quilting, having succumbed to the pleasures of seeing the pattern come alive quickly while requiring little skill. It requires only simple sewing skills whether you choose to stitch by hand or by machine, yet it offers much scope in terms of fabric and thread choices. Designs can be easily adapted from embroidery or quilting patterns by the simple expedient of doubling lines to form channels to be stitched for the cords to be threaded through.

Suitable patterns

Virtually any pattern can be adapted for corded quilting by doubling some or all of its lines, although curved lines generally translate more successfully into cording than patterns which have a high percentage of sharp angles. Having said that, there are always exceptions to any rule! If your appetite for corded quilting is whetted by the projects which follow, you are bound to find ideas and inspiration from many sources such as tiles, carvings, and Celtic knotwork.

How it is done

In corded or Italian quilting the design lines are stitched to form channels which then have a 'cord' – usually a soft yarn – inserted from the reverse of the work to give a strongly sculptured effect. Traditionally the design was marked onto a lightweight fabric, such as muslin, cheesecloth or mull, which was then basted to the top fabric. The design was stitched from the reverse side following the marked lines. Once all the stitching had been completed, lengths of soft yarn

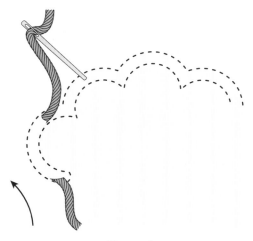

Figure 1

could be threaded through the channels from the reverse side using a bodkin or similar large-eyed, blunt needle to separate the threads of the lightweight backing (Fig 1).

After the main design lines had been corded in this way, further quilting could be added by treating the two layers as one and layering and basting top, batting and backing in the usual way.

If you choose to use running stitch, the above method works well and eliminates the need to remove pattern lines from the top fabric when the stitching is complete. However, if you want to use back, chain or stem stitch to define the channels, you need to mark and work the design on the top fabric, since unlike running stitch, there is a right and a wrong side to each of these stitches. The benefit of working from the top or right side is that you do have a choice of stitch, and for mainly decorative pieces using a different stitch such as chain or back stitch can considerably enhance the sculptured effect of the cording. Many people feel more comfortable working running stitch from the right side as well, and for this reason they

Cording, trapunto and traditional quilting are the techniques used to create this silk cot quilt designed and stitched by Sandie Lush.

mark and stitch on the top fabric. Whatever your choice of stitch, you will be able to start and finish all sewing and cording threads on the reverse or wrong side. A third option, and one which is increasingly preferred, would be to work cording after any other quilting had been completed; in this case the backing fabric may need to be carefully pierced, or even cut, and secured with neat stitching to finish. If you decide to incorporate stippling in a design which also includes cording and trapunto, working the stippling before the cording and stuffing makes it much easier to handle the piece. Some contemporary quilters have become so adept at cording that they have devised ways of piercing the top or backing fabric so that no final securing or neatening of holes or small cuts is required. If you use an ordinary needle and sewing thread to draw the cording yarn into the channels from either side of the work, you may be able coax the

Figure 2

parted fabric threads back into position. At this point I must confess to being a traditionalist. I am not entirely at ease with this approach although it does work extremely well for others. The advantage of this method is that there is no need to stitch around the corded parts of the design a second time if the cording forms only part of the total quilted texture. If you work the cording first and 'other' quilting afterwards as described above, you will find that a second line of stitching through all three layers outside the stitched channels may be needed to give extra clarity and definition (Fig 2). There is no reason why you should not use machine stitching, which will give clear crisp lines with excellent definition, to make the channels for this type of quilting. 'Mock' corded quilting is easily done using the twin needle facility on a machine and stitching through three layers as for ordinary quilting. If you are in a hurry you can stitch right across each point where pattern lines cross; if you have a little more patience, you may prefer to stop and restart at each intersection. Alternatively each line of the channel can be separately machine sewn and then corded using the method described above.

Press the top fabric and decide whether you will work from the back or front – this may be dictated by the type of stitch you want to use or the type of top fabric you have chosen. Mark the pattern onto the appropriate fabric: the top fabric if you will be working from the front, the cheesecloth/muslin if you will be working from the back.

Use a marker which is suitable for the fabric (see page 9). The marker should be easily removable if you will be working from the front, while any marker used on the muslin or back layer needs to be either totally removable or totally fast if the work will eventually be washed – pencil or permanent pen might be a good choice.

Once the pattern is marked out, baste the two fabric layers together so they will not shift as you stitch. Then you are ready to use the thread and stitch of your choice to define the channels of the pattern.

Threads

As corded quilting seems to fall naturally into the decorative rather than strictly functional category of quilting techniques, you can be as adventurous as you wish with your choice of thread. Experiment with using fine cotton perle, coton a broder, or two or more strands of embroidery floss as well as standard sewing or quilting thread. It is not essential to match the thread colour to that of the top fabric, but the overall texture will be enhanced if you choose a thread which is at least two or three shades darker than the fabric.

Yarn for cording

The type of yarn you choose for cording will depend to some extent on what is easily available and the effect you want to achieve. A softly twisted wool yarn specifically for cording is stocked by many quilt shops and haberdashery (notions) departments, but you may prefer to use a finer wool or acrylic knitting yarn to cord very narrow channels. A closely twisted yarn such as knitting cotton, crochet yarn, or coton a broder will work well if your aim is to have strongly defined lines of very narrow cording. Give some thought to the colour of the yarn you choose. The usual choice is white or neutral, but it is often possible to enhance the corded lines by using a yarn that is a deeper tone of the top fabric colour or even a contrasting colour. For example, if your top fabric is white or cream, a deep pink or bright red yarn may show through sufficiently to give the impression of pale pink lines on the front of the work. You could have great fun experimenting, but make sure that the yarn is colourfast before you begin.

Once the stitching is complete, you can begin the cording. Thread a bodkin or large-eyed blunt tapestry needle with a short length – about 18 inches (45cm) of the yarn you have chosen for the cording and either part the threads of the backing fabric with the tip of the needle or make a tiny slit with small sharp scissors. Slide the bodkin along the channel until it becomes difficult to push it any further – probably 5–6 inches (12–15cm) from the starting point, then bring the needle out through the backing fabric. Ease the yarn within the channel by stroking it back with the needle/bodkin tip to ensure that it lies flat rather than bunching up the work, and then re-insert the needle at the point of exit to carry the yarn further along the channel (Fig 3). At the beginning and end of each

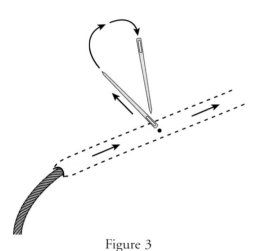

Figure 3

channel, you can either leave a short tail of the yarn which can be folded over and secured with a few herringbone stitches (Fig 4) or you may prefer just to cut the yarn so that it lies exactly within the channel. Of these two options, the first, which allows for some shrinkage of the yarn, is recommended if the finished piece will be subjected to a moderate amount of wear, tear and laundering, whereas the second, which does not allow for yarn shrinkage, is more appropriate if the piece is purely decorative.

If the design you have chosen includes sharp points and tight curves, take care not to pull the yarn too

Figure 4

tightly as you are cording. You may find it helpful to leave a small loop of the yarn exactly on points (Fig 5) and also distributed at intervals around tight curves. Again this allows for settlement and shrinkage of the yarn and ensures that it fits snugly into the channels. As with most other aspects of quilting it is advisable to work systematically when cording, either from one corner to its opposite or outwards from the centre. You may want to add regular quilting and/or trapunto to your design once all the cording is complete.

Figure 5

TRAPUNTO

Trapunto, or stuffed quilting, is a popular choice to accompany corded quilting and can be worked at the same stage. This involves making a small slit from the back of the work and adding extra batting to the selected shape(s) (Fig 6a) and closing the slit with a few stitches (Fig 6b).

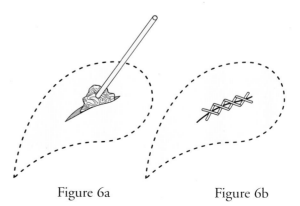

Figure 6a   Figure 6b

Like corded quilting, trapunto or stuffed quilting can be worked using a top fabric and a lightweight backing fabric such as cheesecloth or muslin, stitching and then stuffing the pattern shapes from the reverse side of the work (see page 53) before or after adding further quilting. Judicious use of the trapunto technique can add considerable emphasis to specific areas of a design and more than justifies the additional time it requires.

Depending on the nature of the project, you could dispense with the second layer of lightweight fabric and quilt the entire design first, adding the stuffing from the reverse side through small slits made in the backing fabric and possibly even parting the batting layer to allow the extra pieces of stuffing to be pushed through to the very front of the work. This will give excellent definition and 'loft' to the stuffed shapes but of course means that the backing fabric is cut and therefore must later be neatly secured with stitches. If the backing fabric is relatively loosely woven, it may be possible to ease very tiny pieces of stuffing through from the back working between the threads – this will avoid any cutting and securing but can be mind-numbingly slow to work.

In the past few years, quilters have been looking at several slightly different ways of working trapunto and have been questioning the traditional methods. John Flynn's work, for example, often includes close quilting and trapunto, and he advocates sliding the extra batting into a partially stitched shape between the layers and from the side rather than the back. Sue Rodgers recommends using a weaver's needle, which is long and flat, to introduce lengths of yarn into the stitched shape, and she takes the needle between the fabric threads rather than slitting the fabric itself. You may find that using the traditional method works best in the beginning and you can then experiment for yourself later on.

If trapunto is used in conjunction with traditional quilting, the shapes will probably have been defined with running stitch before they are stuffed, but this is by no means the only stitch suitable for this technique. As with corded quilting you could consider stem, back or chain stitch using either matching or slightly darker-coloured threads of various types and thickness.

If you plan to use all three quilting techniques in the same piece, it may be simpler to work the traditional quilting as the final stage, treating the top fabric and lightweight backing as a single layer and then putting three layers together in the usual way. This means that all starting and finishing for the corded

and trapunto sections will be covered by the batting and new backing fabric.

Traditionally trapunto has been handstitched, but there is no reason why it cannot be done on a sewing machine. Mark the complete design on the top fabric in the usual way, add a layer of batting underneath and then stitch through both layers around any areas you wish to emphasise.

Turn the work over and carefully cut away the batting close to the stitching (Fig 7). Now layer the stitched top fabric with batting and backing into the usual 'sandwich' and baste using either safety pins or plastic tags before continuing with any additional quilting. This method is highly effective and, if you are comfortable with free machine quilting, remarkably quick. Of course there is no need to limit yourself to just one extra layer. You could stitch and cut several successive layers before adding the final batting and backing to achieve a highly sculpted appearance. But bear in mind this small note of caution, though: the more layers there are, the greater the possibilities for distortion.

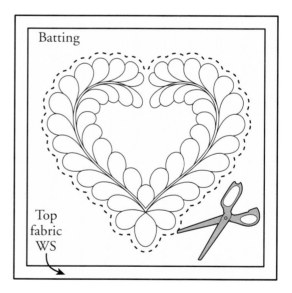

Figure 7

Alongside the revival of interest in cording and stuffing techniques, there has been an increased willingness to indulge in closely spaced elaborate quilting, which often makes a gorgeous accompaniment to either or both techniques. Stipple quilting, perhaps the ultimate in closely spaced quilting, is a technique which more and more quilters are experimenting with, and the results are frequently stunning. In the dim and distant past stippling was defined as closely packed quilting stitches, none of which run in exactly the same direction (Fig 8). (If you try this method, you will find that it is very slow and requires considerable reserves of patience and perseverance.) Then along came American quilter John Flynn with a fresh approach which made the whole process infinitely simpler and a little faster to work! Instead of trying to change the direction of each stitch taken, Flynn recommends dividing the area to be stippled into regular sections, by creating an imaginary grid over your design.

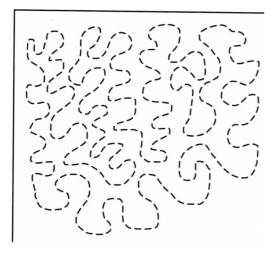

Figure 8

These sections can then be stitched one at a time, filling in the area with closely spaced short lines of quilting, either lining up the stitches to form a subtle secondary pattern as in Fig 9 or deliberately offsetting the stitches to keep the texture more random in

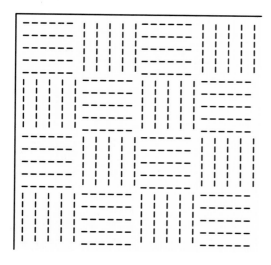

Figure 9

appearance (Fig 10). And what of stippling by machine? You can certainly achieve a densely textured effect with 'scribble' or meander quilting, but it is not possible to truly replicate the subtle secondary patterns of hand stippling. However, if your project calls simply for contrasts in texture, the machine is an excellent option.

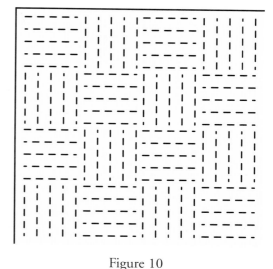

Figure 10

If you surround a quilted design with a completely stippled or densely quilted background, you will probably find that the contrast in density of quilting between the main and background areas gives the overall appearance of trapunto.

Be aware of the potential in all three techniques for distorting your work – cording can leave puckers, stuffing can further add to puckering from cording, and stippling may control puckers from first two techniques but may leave ripples at outside edges. If, despite your best efforts, you find that there are ripples, a few 'controlling' lines as in Fig 11 worked around the edges may help to ease some of this fullness.

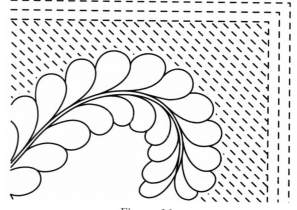

Figure 11

CORDED AND STUFFED CUSHION

This cushion had trapunto or stuffing added to the main design areas and was completed with diagonal lines of quilting worked through additional batting and backing. You may prefer to use the cording technique on its own, in which case your finished piece will resemble the cushion shown on page 58, which uses the same basic pattern but is not stuffed and has the four outer loops eliminated.

the cushion shown on page 58

YOU WILL NEED

20-inch (50cm) square of top fabric
20-inch (50cm) square of open-weave muslin (cheesecloth)
22-inch (55cm) square of fabric for cushion back
¼ yard (0.25m) plain or print fabric for borders – optional
Hank of soft quilting wool or yarn of your choice
Large-eyed blunt tapestry needle or bodkin
Thread several tones darker than top fabric
Sharps or betweens needles
Tapestry needle or bodkin
Tracing paper and medium black marker pen
Fabric marker (a water-soluble crayon two shades darker than the top fabric might be a good choice)

Finished size: 15 inches (38cm) square without borders, 19 inches (48cm) with borders

Opposite: Cording, trapunto and traditional quilting are featured in this cushion.

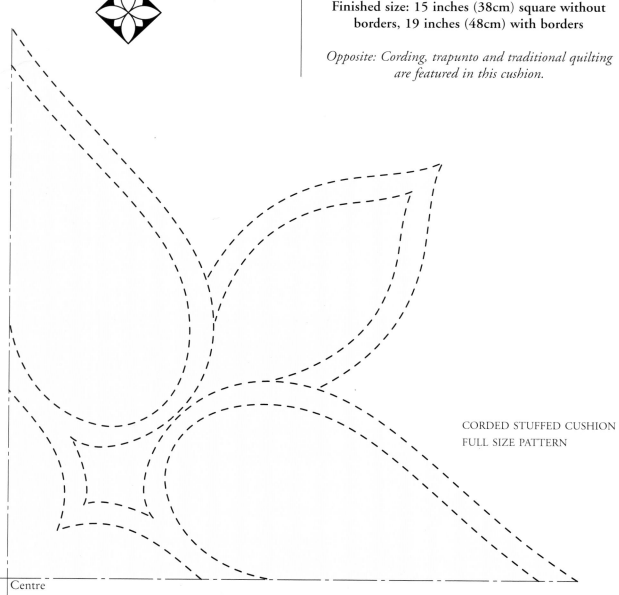

CORDED STUFFED CUSHION
FULL SIZE PATTERN

Centre

1   Trace the quarter pattern on page 56 four times to produce the complete design and go over the outlines with a black marker.

If you have chosen a pale-coloured fabric you will be able to trace the design through using a marker of your choice – for dark fabrics you could use a light box (see page 10) and a pale coloured marker.

2   Baste together the marked top fabric and muslin.

3   Stitch all the marked lines of the design with the stitch and thread of your choice – running stitch is a good beginning. You may want to try using backstitch although it may take a little practice to get a really smooth-looking line.

4   Now it's time to start cording. Turn the work to the wrong side, thread a bodkin or blunt needle with a shortish length of quilting wool or the yarn you have chosen.

Begin cording at the centre and work to the outside edges of design, remembering that key word 'systematic'. Take care not to tug quickly or strongly on the cording yarn as you ease it through the channels, as this can distort the top fabric. Make sure the cord lies easily and flat within the channel, with no puckering visible on the right side. One way of reducing potential puckers is to ease the cheesecloth/muslin back from direction of cording with the tip of your needle or fingernail. Leave tiny loops at each exit point if you wish and remember also to leave a loop at each

Simple cording without additional quilting still looks effective.

sharp point (see page 53). Make sure the points are filled with cord by taking the tip of the needle to the far side of each point before withdrawing it to leave a loop. The first round of cording at the centre of the pattern is shown in Fig 12, with the position of the entry and exit holes, and the second cording sequence is marked to show where loops should be left at the entry/exit holes.

Try not to turn your work over before the cording is complete. The process does not take long and is wonderfully effective when done.

5   Any further quilting can be done once all the cording is finished – layer up for quilting as usual by treating the two fabrics as a new top fabric, and then basting and quilting. Remember that you will get a crisper definition of the main design if you work a line of quilting close to the original stitching lines of the channels.

6   Make up a cushion using your preferred method. Printed fabric borders have been added to the example shown, or you could, of course, use a toning plain fabric.

Figure 12

FEATHERED HEART CUSHION

This traditional-style quilting pattern adapts very well for trapunto work and would make a charming wedding cushion. The instructions given below are for hand stitching, but this project could easily be done by machine using the technique described on page 54.

YOU WILL NEED

18-inch (45cm) square of top fabric (this could be a fancy fabric such as satin or silk)
18-inch (45cm) square of lightweight batting
18-inch (45cm) square of cheesecloth/muslin (if you are working in the traditional way)
20-inch (50cm) square of fabric for the cushion back
Scraps of standard 2-ounce batting cut into tiny pieces for stuffing
Small sharp scissors
Cocktail stick or similar for pushing batting into place
Sewing or quilting thread one or two shades darker than the top fabric
Quilting needle of your choice

Finished size: 16 inches (40cm) square

1   Trace the half pattern on page 62 twice to complete the heart design and go over the pencil outline with a black marker.

2   Mark the design onto your top fabric – tracing through (see page 10) would be the simplest way if your fabric is pale enough. There is no need to mark the lines for the crosshatched section; this can easily be done later using masking tape (see pages 10–11). If you have chosen a fine or slippery top fabric, it may be easier to mark these lines with tape at the quilting stage rather than marking lines beforehand onto a mobile fabric and trying to avoid inaccuracies.

3   Baste the top fabric and backing together.

4   Stitch the complete design. Remember that there are a number of stitches which you can use. Stitch the spine of the feather first (Fig 13a), then work the feather space systematically either from top to bottom or bottom to top (Fig 13b).

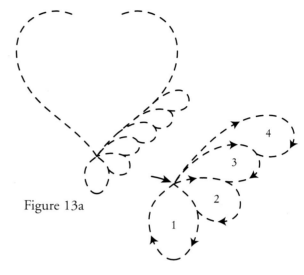

Figure 13a

Figure 13b

5   Stuff the trapunto spaces. It is probably best to work first on one side of spine, then the other, and so on. Take care not to overstuff each shape and keep the stuffing evenly distributed within each loop. Checking the front of the work from time to time will help you avoid any problems.

6   Once you are satisfied that all loops are evenly filled, continue with standard quilting for the crosshatched section in the middle of the heart and add any quilting you wish to do on the outer background.

7   Make a cushion using your preferred method. Piping or a frill might be a pleasing finishing touch for this project.

A traditional-style feathered heart pattern is an excellent subject for trapunto.

FEATHERED HEART CUSHION FULL SIZE PATTERN

Centre

CHAPTER FOUR

Machine Quilting

Machine quilting is not a late twentieth-century phenomenon. Examples of machine quilting from 1875 onwards are not difficult to find and some are surprisingly complex, given the basic nature of the early sewing machines. It is difficult for us to comprehend the overwhelming impact of the sewing machine now that we have grown accustomed to the facilities and gadgetry of today's machines, but in the last quarter of the nineteenth century it must have offered a wonderful release from the drudgery of plain sewing. Many owners would no doubt have exploited the potential of this new tool to the full, including patchwork and quilting.

In the first few years of the current quilting revival which began in the early 1970s, machine quilting aroused little interest. We were all too busy rediscovering the joys of handwork. Using a sewing machine to speed up the piecing process soon became acceptable but 'real' quilting continued to be done by hand. So the stage was set for the advent of machine quilting – more and more patchwork projects needing to be quilted, more ideas and less time. Add to this constant improvements to the machines themselves and it makes a potent brew. Gradually the realisation dawned that there would never be enough time during the average quilter's lifespan to finish even a quarter of the projects just begging to be made. Consequently more attention was paid to practising the skills of machine quilting, so that now machine quilting is not only accepted, but is done increasingly frequently and well by an ever-increasing number of quilters.

As someone who never excelled at practical needlework and who nursed an unhealthy fear of sewing machines, I was a late convert to machine quilting. I admired the skill of others, but felt it was a technique I would never be able to master simply because it involved close contact and familiarity with a sewing machine. Then the day came when there were simply too many unfinished and never-even-started projects because of the time needed to quilt them (my nephew's going-to-college quilt is one example; he has now graduated and the quilt is still a figment of my imagination). To begin with I acquired a walking foot for my machine and outline-quilted several patchwork blocks to make into cushions, discovering along the way that this sort of machine quilting is easier than I thought and great for getting things finished. This gave me the confidence to try free machine quilting. My first attempts were not wonderful, but practice made a considerable difference to both my skills and confidence. In the light of this anecdotal background I have devised simple practical projects for this section to give you practice and confidence in developing your own machine quilting skills.

BASIC MACHINE QUILTING

There are two basic requirements for successful machine quilting. The first is access to a sewing machine and the second is practice and the determination to succeed. In this latter respect machine quilting is identical to hand quilting although of course the results are different – machine quilting gives crisper and more sharply defined lines than the running stitch of hand quilting.

Let's look first at what you will need from your sewing machine. The most fundamental thing is that it should be clean, oiled and in good running order. You can arrive at this commendable state of affairs by either locating and consulting the handbook and following the instructions for general maintenance therein, or by contacting a reputable service company and giving them the problem to deal with. Either way it is worth taking the time and effort to make sure that your machine is in good running order and stays that way with regular cleaning.

The age and make of the machine matters far less than you might think, although many of the new machines have all sorts of endearing and ingenious features designed to make your sewing life virtually effortless. Check the handbook to see if it is possible to drop or cover the feed dogs on the machine – these are the toothed strips on the bed of the machine immediately under the presser foot whose purpose is to feed the fabric under the foot to the needle. Dropping or covering them reduces the traction on fabric being stitched so that you can move it around easily, which is what you will be doing in free machine quilting. If it is not possible to drop or cover the feed dogs (and on all but the most ancient of models it is usually possible to do one or the other), you may still be able to free machine quilt by removing the presser foot before stitching.

A sewing machine driven by electricity or foot-treadle power, which means that you have both hands free to move the fabric layers around, will be easier to use for free machine quilting work than a purely manual model, although it is amazing what can be achieved with sufficient determination!

Invest in a walking or even-feed foot suitable for your machine – it will enable you to do all sorts of simple quilting patterns from straight lines to shallow curves without any need for dropping or covering the feed dogs. You will also find all sorts of other uses for a walking foot once you have acquired one. Because it feeds the fabric(s) evenly under the needle, it is an immensely helpful attachment for adding quilt bindings and even for straightforward piecing where accuracy is paramount. Also look in the box of machine accessories (you put it in a safe place, remember?) to see if you have a darning foot. If not, try to acquire one to use in free machine quilting.

Equipped with a smooth running machine, walking foot and knowledge of feed dog dropping or covering, you are ready to look at the other requirements for machine quilting.

A good supply of machine needles is probably the next essential. Far too many of us are guilty of changing machine needles only when we notice that there are odd clunking noises as we sew. Try to acquire the habit of changing to a new needle for each project and you will be helping your machine to help you, as well as supporting a vital section of the quilting industry. The brand of needle you use is a personal choice based on what is available; the most frequently used size of needle for machine quilting is a 14/90 or its equivalent. You could also try a jeans needle, which has a long, relatively fine point.

Thread

Because the top thread is more visible in machine quilting than in hand quilting, colour choice assumes more importance. If you look at the waistcoat on page 71, you will see that the use of a variegated thread gives considerable impact to the simple quilting design. If you choose thread to tone with your top fabric, it will leave the texture to speak for itself; if you contrast the thread and fabric colours, you will add to the texture – the possibilities are endless. Experiment with different types of thread to see which ones suit your machine best – try as many as you can from the vast selection available. It may be helpful to use a slightly lighter-weight thread for the top so that it is pulled through the quilt layers by the heavier bobbin thread. 'Invisible' thread is a fine nylon monofilament which has been a popular choice with many machine quilters over the past few years. Once you have gained a little experience with this type of thread, which contributes texture only, you may feel sufficiently confident to change to 'ordinary' or non-transparent thread to add a little extra impact. On the other hand you may decide that the transparent thread gives the effect you want and not feel any need to switch – like so many other aspects of quilting, it is all a matter of trying things for yourself and following your own preferences.

Fabrics

With care and that other vital ingredient, practice, it is possible to machine quilt virtually any fabric, although you will probably want to avoid heavy tweeds and very delicate silks.

Battings

Machine quilting seems to work best on a dense lightweight batting of cotton or cotton/polyester blend. The choice and quality of battings continue to improve almost monthly and several suppliers offer a sampling service which will give you an opportunity to try different types before deciding which one will be best for a particular project.

Suitable patterns

If you are new to machine quilting it is a good idea to gain confidence and practice by limiting yourself to very simple patterns to begin with. Straight lines and shallow curves can be done using a walking foot, which means that you can do crosshatching and some cable patterns as well as outline quilting on patchwork.

When you are free machine quilting with the darning foot and feed dogs lowered or covered, start with patterns which require a minimum of starting, stopping and finishing off – known as continuous line patterns. The tremendous increase in the popularity of machine quilting means that there is now an excellent choice of continuous line patterns available either in stencil or printed form. In addition, it is often possible, with only minimal adjustments, to adapt traditional or other patterns into continuous lines suitable for machine quilting.

Marking patterns

Marking the pattern onto the fabric is much the same for machine quilting as for hand quilting – the lines need to be visible and easily removable. However, because of the differences in working and handling machine quilting, there is one easy way of marking which you might like to try. Mark the complete pattern on lightweight tracing paper and pin or secure it in position over the top of the work. Stitching along the marked lines will perforate the paper and when you've finished, tear the paper away. Hey presto, there are no markings to remove from the fabric.

Preparing the layers

There is no substitute for good preparation. Much of the ultimate success of a piece depends on how well the three layers have been put together – this is just a formal way of saying that you are going to have to baste the layers before you can quilt them. Stitch basting is one possibility, but the stitches may get caught under the foot; lots of small safety pins are a popular alternative. Straight pins have a distressing knack of working loose and also scratching your hands. The relatively new basting guns (see page 12) which 'shoot' plastic tags through the layers may be the answer to the machine (and even hand) quilters' prayer, offering ease, speed and accuracy in basting. Despite an ongoing debate regarding damage to fabric from these guns, I find that the holes made by the needle of the gun I use – there are of course slight differences between the brands available – are no larger than those made with safety pins and the timesaving factor is so dramatic that I now consider the gun mightier than the needle or safety pin for basting. Whichever method you choose, bear in mind that the basting needs to be close and evenly spaced, exactly as for hand quilting.

For large projects such as bed-sized quilts it is near impossible to manipulate and juggle the acres of cloth under the needle without losing first your temper and then your general sense of direction. Far better to take extra time at the preparation stage to roll and package large projects so that only a very limited and manageable area is left exposed and ready to stitch. Use bicycle clips or lengths of masking tape to secure the rolls temporarily while you quilt one section. Then unclip, re-roll and quilt the next section. If you are working in a limited space on a large project, even this roll and package preparation may be cumbersome as you manipulate a rolled quilt that seems to take on a life of its own. Experienced machine wizards report good results from just 'making a nest', that is having a small area to be quilted smoothed out under the machine's foot and the remaining bulk of the quilt loosely heaped up on all sides. When it is time to move on, a fresh area is smoothed out.

Organisation of workspace

This sounds alarmingly grand but only means that you should give some thought to location when you get ready for machine quilting. If the bed of the machine can easily be made level with the surrounding table/work area, that will be ideal. Certainly you will find it helpful to have additional work space to the back and side of your machine to support large pieces of work, and it would be wise to sit on a back-friendly chair so that you are at a comfortable working height with good support for your back. Please don't rely solely on the machine itself for illumination – you will be concentrating on your work at close quarters and a strong, well-aimed light is a must.

Make a practice piece

So now you're ready to begin quilting. The machine is all set, workspace organised, pattern marked out, thread chosen, basting accomplished. Why then bother to stop and make a practice piece? The answer is that you can eliminate unforeseen problems on a practice piece, particularly if you use the same fabrics and batting and method of basting for your practice piece (or scribble cloths as they are more irreverently known) as those used for your project. A scribble cloth gives you a chance to check your tension, thread and pattern before committing to the real thing, and anyone who has tried unpicking more than a few stitches of machine quilting will confirm that, like pattern marking, it is far better to test first rather than plunge in armed only with hope. Using a scribble cloth also gives you a chance to warm up and get the feel of machine quilting, and if you are new to machine quilting I suggest spending several hours (not all at one sitting) just doodling and experimenting on a scribble cloth to get familiar with the whole process and acquire that elusive confidence.

Adjusting the tension

What is a correct tension? For most machine quilting you really want to have the top and bottom threads locking somewhere in the middle of the batting rather than on the top or reverse side of the work. So use your scribble cloth to check the appearance of the stitch. If you can see 'blobs' of the bobbin thread on the top side, or dots of the top thread on the under-side of the work, you need to adjust the tension fractionally until the problem goes away. On many machines only the top thread tension can be altered, but on those where both top and bobbin tension can be changed, try different top tension settings first before tampering with the bobbin tension. The hand-book that you found when dealing with cleaning and oiling your machine should explain where to locate the tension mechanisms, how many there are, and give a guide to standard settings.

The stitch itself

If you are using a walking foot, the simplest way to start is to set your stitch length to 'very short' or zero and make a few stitches at this setting, after which you can gradually increase the stitch length to the length you have chosen during your scribble cloth experiments. To finish off a line of quilting, gradually decrease the stitch length again over the last inch (2.5cm) or so until you arrive back at zero. Then take a few stitches at this setting. The tiny stitches at the start and finish of the line hold the thread in place and are robust in wear – if you ever need to unpick them you will see why this is a good way to start and finish. The threads can just be clipped away, both front and back, or you may prefer to pull the top thread through to the back and knot them together before clipping.

Just a brief warning about stitch direction when using a walking foot – you will get better results if you work all lines in the same direction rather than turning around and working alternate lines the opposite way (Fig 1). Working in one direction reduces the potential ripple factor between the lines because the fabric is always pushed slightly ahead of the needle as you stitch.

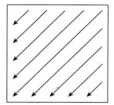

Figure 1

For free machine quilting, starting and finishing is broadly similar to that described above, except that you are in charge of the stitch length – once the feed dogs have been dropped or covered, it is no longer the machine which determines the length of stitch but the speed at which the fabric is moved under the needle. You could just clip the starting and finishing threads or take them through to the reverse side as described above, but for this particular quilting method it may help to reduce potential tangles if you draw the bobbin thread through to the top of the work and hold both it and the top thread to the back of the needle while you take the first few stitches before clipping them.

Free machine quilting

When you work without the feed dogs operating, you are able to move your work around freely under the needle, so the sky is the limit in terms of the possibilities of this technique. But you will need to practice (that dreadful word again). It sounds easy enough and if you have the chance to see an accomplished machine quilter at work, it certainly looks easy enough. However, don't expect show-winning results immediately, and give yourself plenty of time trying out basic meandering and curved line patterns. First try and keep the machine speed constant and even, probably somewhere between half and full speed. Then concentrate on moving the scribble cloth around smoothly, without too much jerking and pulling, by keeping your hands on either side of the needle and using them to move the fabric in various directions. Think of a fixed pencil and pretend you are drawing a picture by moving a sheet of paper around underneath it. This will give you some idea of what free machine quilting is all about – it is the fabric, not the needle, movement which is all-important.

Once you acquire a little confidence in your ability to keep the machine running and the fabric moving, you might try the often recommended exercise of quilting your name on the scribble cloth – apparently once you can do this, you are well on the way to developing your machine quilting skills!

DIAMOND-IN-SQUARE CUSHION

The quilted cushion shown on the left on page 69, could be made on any machine using either a walking or even-feed foot, or just the normal presser foot, and is an ideal beginner's project.

YOU WILL NEED

24-inch (60cm) square of top fabric
24-inch (60cm) square of backing fabric
24-inch (60cm) square of lightweight needlepunched batting
24-inch (60cm) square of fabric for the cushion back
Sewing thread – a contrasting variegated thread was used for this example
Sewing machine in good working order (clean – i.e. fluff-free – and oiled and with new needle)
Walking or even-feed foot (NB if this type of foot is not available for your machine, slacken the top pressure slightly and use the standard presser foot)
Fabric marker
Ruler
Plenty of small safety pins – minimum 20

Finished size: 18 inches (46cm) square

1   Find the centre of the fabric square and mark it lightly. Measure 8 inches (20cm) from centre both horizontally and vertically and connect these four points with your marker in straight lines to form a square on point (Fig 2). Mark the edges of the outer square, then measure and mark lines in both the centre square and the outer triangles using the photograph overleaf as a guide. You do not have to follow this arrangement exactly – Fig 3 shows an alternative.

2   Use small safety pins to baste the three layers together, working from the centre to the outside edges in either a sunburst or grid formation (see page 11).

3   Begin stitching the straight lines from the centre following the sequence suggested in Fig 4. Begin with

short stitches, lengthen them and finish with short stitches again, and clip both top and bobbin threads to leave about 2 inches (5cm) free so that they can be taken through to the wrong side and tied off later.

4   When the quilting is complete, check that all the ends have been tied and/or clipped off before making a cushion using your preferred method.

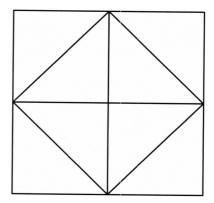

Figure 2

Figure 3

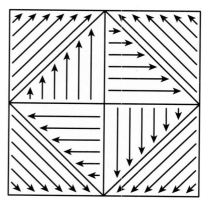

Figure 4

SAMPLER CUSHION

Try this project as an easy introduction to the technique of free machine quilting once you have played with a scribble cloth.

YOU WILL NEED

24-inch (60cm) square of top fabric
24-inch (60cm) square of lightweight batting
24-inch (60cm) square of backing fabric
24-inch (60cm) square of fabric for the back of the cushion
Sewing thread (a contrasting variegated thread was used)
Sewing machine (still in good working order as for the previous project, and with the feed dogs capable of being dropped or covered)
Darning foot for your machine
Walking or even-feed foot for your machine
Safety pins for basting
Fabric marker

Finished size: 18 inches (26cm) square

1   Mark out a 20-inch (50cm) square on your top fabric; this should leave 2 inches (5cm) on all sides.

Mark at least three lines within this square as shown in Fig 5 to divide it into diagonal bands. The bands do not have to be of equal width, and you can have more than three bands if you wish.

2   Using the walking foot and with the feed dogs up, quilt the framework lines you have just marked i.e. the diagonal lines and the square. You can stitch either single or double lines – double lines as shown will give a subtle emphasis to the overall effect and can either be marked onto the fabric before you begin to quilt or you can judge them 'by eye' after working the single lines.

3   Now you can fill in the bands with free machine patterns of your choice. Drop or cover the feed dogs and change to the darning foot. You can follow the pattern suggestions (Fig 6) and stitching sequences (Fig 7) or use any other ideas you may have – other suggestions are shown in Figs 8 and 9. In less time than you would have thought possible, you will have a quilted piece ready to make up into a cushion!

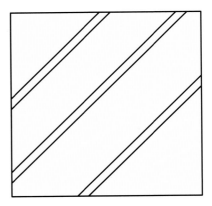

Figure 5

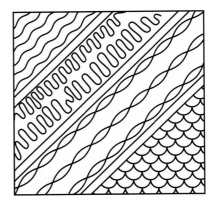

Figure 6

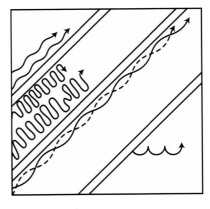

Figure 7

These two cushions have simple machine quilting and are ideal beginning projects.

Figure 8

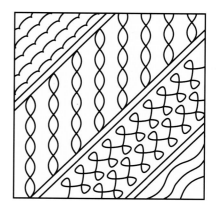

Figure 9

MEANDERING
DAISIES
WAISTCOAT

You don't have to be a machine quilting expert to make this waistcoat – the daisy design is quick and easy to do. It would look equally good in pale or dark fabric with toning or matching threads – a variegated metallic thread was used for this example.

YOU WILL NEED

1 yard (1m) of fabric for top
(this amount is sufficient for making front facings if you need them)
1 yard (1m) of fabric for backing
1 yard (1m) of fabric for lining (optional)
1 yard (1m) of lightweight needlepunched batting
Coloured or metallic thread
Waistcoat pattern of your choice
Small safety pins or needle and thread for basting

1   The waistcoat is worked as one large rectangle, then cut to shape afterwards.

The quilting pattern requires no marking as it is easier to achieve a random look without marking so you can layer the top batting and backing ready for basting immediately. You may find it helpful when you come to do the quilting if you stitch-baste (against all previous advice) for this particular project. You will then have clearly marked lines within which to work the daisy pattern (Fig 10) without fear of the lines of daisies drifting too far off course. Alternatively, pin-baste with safety pins, keeping the pins aligned in rows.

2   Mark the starting edge with a safety pin or knot of coloured thread. This will remind you to work all lines in the same direction. Approach the whole project as a way of creating texture at random and don't worry about 'getting it right' – plunge in and enjoy yourself. Fig 11 shows a suggested stitching route for the daisy pattern. The basic circling motion which forms the daisies is shown in Fig 12 opposite. You may work four or six loops per daisy. Expert Sally Radway followed my choice of five loops when she quilted this piece.

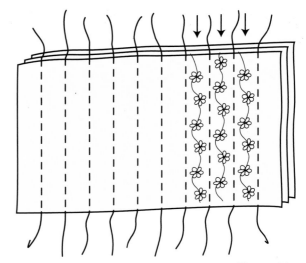

Figure 10

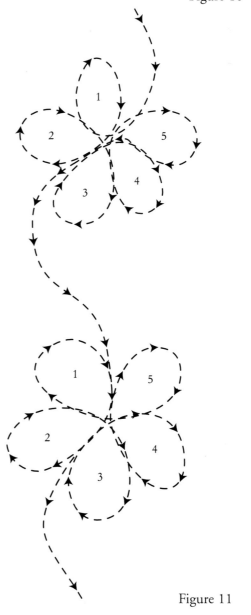

Figure 11

3   Once you have covered the large rectangle with line after line of meandering daisies, take a moment to admire your work before going on to cut out and make up the waistcoat. If making garments is not your forte, or you would prefer to do the quilting for another project, then find an unsuspecting friend who has dressmaking skills and will do a deal. Otherwise, you can treat the quilted rectangle as fabric and pin your pattern pieces in position in the usual way. Lining the waistcoat will give a good finish and also takes care of the raw edges, but if you are in too much of a rush to cut and sew a lining, you will have to take the time you thought you had saved to bind all the raw edges. It's probably faster (and simpler) to make a lining and finish the edge with a line of topstitching.

Machine quilted waistcoat by Maggie Alexander, quilted by Sally Radway.

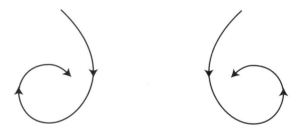

Figure 12

MACHINE QUILTED STRIPPY

This simple strippy quilt could be quilted using either the walking foot or free machine quilting. Although it was designed as an exercise in free machine technique, it could be done relatively easily using a walking foot since the curves are long and shallow.

YOU WILL NEED

¾ yard (0.75m) of apricot fabric
¾ yard (0.75m) of cream fabric
1½ yards (1.5m) backing fabric
Lightweight needlepunched batting to measure 38 x 48 inches (96 x 121cm)
½ yard (0.5m) fabric for binding (optional)
Thread to tone with each of the 2 main fabrics
Safety pins or basting gun
Fabric marker
Tracing paper and black marker pen

Finished size: 36 x 46 inches (91 x 116cm)

1   Trace the patterns on page 75 and use them to construct a Master Sheet (see page 11) of the quilt on lightweight or tracing paper. Depending on your fabric, you can then either trace through onto the quilt top (see page 10) or pin the plan to the top of the quilt layers as a stitching guide (see page 11).

2   Cut three strips to measure 6 x 44 inches (15 x 111cm) from one of your fabrics and four strips of the same measurement from the second fabric.

3   Seam the strips together using a standard ¼ inch (0.5cm) seam and alternating the direction of the seams as in Fig 13, page 74 to avoid any distortion of the strips. Press the seams towards the darker strips to avoid any showthrough on the right side.

4   Mark the pattern on the quilt top. If you use the trace-through method (see page 10), you can mark one strip at a time, taking care to keep the pattern in the centre of the strip. (You can, if you wish, pin the

This appealing small strippy quilt was machine quilted by Sally Radway.

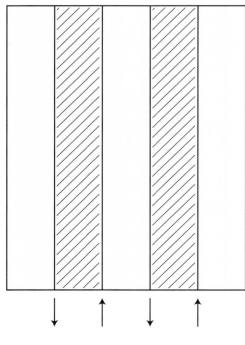

Figure 13

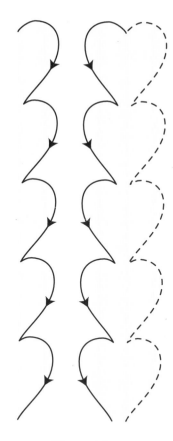

Figure 14a

Master Sheet to the top of the quilt layers and stitch through it – see page 11.)

5 Spread out the three layers and baste them together.

6 You might like to spend a minute or two planning a stitching route for the pattern – one suggestion involving four easy-to-sew lines is shown in Figs 14a and 14b. This route begins at the same edge of the quilt each time. If you are comfortable with machine quilting you could, if you preferred, simply turn around at the end of the first line (Fig 14a). and work the second line (Fig 14b) in the opposite direction without stopping and finishing off threads. With care, it is possible to complete both the large and small heart patterns with only one start and finish per strip. Neither of these two suggested routes is more correct than the other – if you have some machine quilting experience, you will probably feel confident about the non-stop route, whereas the first route may be a little easier for a beginner in that it requires less movement and turning of the quilt under the machine.

Quilt one strip at a time following your chosen route. You could begin with the centre strip and work systematically to the outer edges or you might prefer to work from one edge to the other – as always, the key is to be systematic.

7 When you have finished quilting all the main lines of the design, feel free to add any extra quilting you wish before trimming all three layers flush and binding the edges (see page 17).

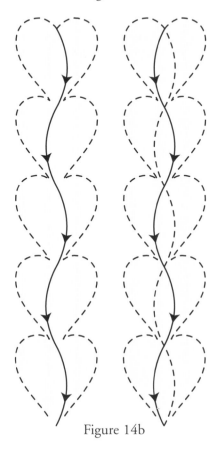

Figure 14b

MACHINE QUILTED STRIPPY PATTERN – enlarge by 125%

ORIENTAL LILAC CUSHION

This continuous line pattern has an Eastern air and makes a generously sized cushion.

YOU WILL NEED

24-inch (60cm) square of top fabric
24-inch (60cm) square of thin needlepunched batting
24-inch (60cm) square of backing fabric
24-inch (60cm) square of fabric for back of cushion
Sewing thread to tone with the top fabric
Safety pins or basting gun
Fabric marker
Tracing or greaseproof paper and black felt marker
Sewing machine with darning foot and feed dogs dropped or covered
A little confidence and practice

Finished size: 20 inches (51cm) square

Centre

ORIENTAL LILAC CUSHION PATTERN – enlarge by 152%

Opposite: An air of the Orient in this machine quilted cushion, stitched by Sally Radway.

1 Trace the patterns on page 76 to make a Master Sheet of the central motif and border (the dotted lines on the patterns indicate where the pattern repeats) and go over the traced lines with black marker. If you wish, add some straight lines as indicated by the dashed lines on the pattern to further define the central and border areas of the design.

2 Using the marking method most appropriate to your fabric, transfer the design to the fabric (see pages 9–11).

3 Baste the three layers together and check your stitch tension (page 66) and warm up on a scribble cloth (page 65) before starting to quilt.

4 A suggested stitching sequence is shown in Fig 15. You may by now have enough confidence and expertise to stitch straight lines without recourse to the walking foot, so if you have added the straight lines it is not absolutely essential to change from the darning foot to a walking foot.

5 When all the quilting is complete, trim the edges of the cushion front as necessary and then make a cushion using your preferred method.

Figure 15

CHAPTER FIVE

Sashiko and Kantha Quilting

SASHIKO

Sashiko, or Japanese quilting as it is sometimes referred to, has caught the imagination of many Western quilters at different times over the past ten or fifteen years. Sashiko developed from a simple darning technique where lines of stitching in a soft thick thread were used to strengthen and reinforce work garments. Gradually the traditional linear patterns so prevalent in Japanese culture were incorporated and the contrast of using a white or natural coloured thread on indigo dyed fabric was exploited to the full.

For anyone who has wrestled with small needles, batting, hoops and frames, sashiko has many delights to offer, not least of which is that it is worked with a large-eyed long needle and usually only two layers of cloth. It is thus immensely portable and easy to do. The impact of this flat quilting technique relies on the contrast between thread and fabric and the subtle texture created by the arrangement of lines and motifs worked in large even stitches. The size of the stitch, traditionally defined as being the same length as a grain of rice, comes as a revelation and comfort to those quilters who have fallen prey to the myth that all stitches should be as small as possible. Making even-sized stitches is not always as easy as it sounds, and sashiko offers the opportunity to develop a practical understanding of what 'even' looks and feels like. It is worth noting here that the definition of 'even' is that the thread forming the stitch on top of the work should appear to be of the same length as the spaces between the stitches.

The temptation to create tiny sub-patterns within the main patterns as they are stitched is almost irresistible. Where lines of stitching cross each other or have the same starting point, secondary patterns can be created by lining up and spacing stitches carefully.

They are fascinating and absorbing to work and add tremendously to the overall effect.

When planning a piece of sashiko quilting you can make individual templates from plastic or thin card to mark around directly onto the fabric. Alternatively you might prefer to put together a complete design arrangement on tracing or greaseproof paper first and then use a light box to mark the full design onto your fabric. For simple straight line patterns you may find it quicker just to rule them directly onto the fabric using a light-coloured marker (see page 9).

Once the complete design is marked onto the fabric, you will need to baste the two layers together to keep them from shifting as they are handled during stitching. You can baste in the usual way or use small safety pins to secure the layers as for machine quilting (see page 11). In either case the basting needs to be no more than 3–4 inches apart (8–10cm).

Needles and threads

If you have experienced moments of frustration with the short small needles traditionally used for hand quilting (and who hasn't?), you are sure to find sashiko a welcome change. Long needles with a clearly visible eye and thick thread make for fast and easy stitching once you have adjusted to the difference. If you have difficulty finding special sashiko needles (which are available at many quilt shops), then a large darning needle will make a good substitute. Some quilt shops also stock skeins of sashiko thread, a soft twist white cotton broadly equivalent to #5 or #8 perle cotton or thick coton a broder. It is not essential to use white thread, but there should be a strong contrast between the colour of the thread and the fabric. Dark threads on pale fabric do not work as well as pale threads on strongly coloured or dark fabrics – the traditional combination of white thread on indigo or navy fabric is used in the projects in this section.

Start and finish

Sashiko is worked with a simple running stitch. You can begin by trailing the thread between the two layers into a position where it will be crossed by a subsequent line of stitching. Popping a knot through the layers, as you would for hand quilting, is not always a satisfactory option when you are using a thick thread although it may be possible and is worth trying. Sometimes, long starting threads can be left trailing beyond the starting point from between the two layers which can later be knotted together into a simple tassel. All the starting threads in a fan design can be secured in this way, for example, with a new thread used for each row. Unlike traditional Western quilting, sashiko does not have to be completely reversible, so if you wish you can begin with a knot on the reverse of the work, finish off by trailing threads between the two layers, and then weave back along two or three stitches on the reverse (Fig 1).

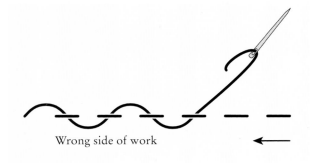

Wrong side of work

Figure 1

Size of stitch

It is worth emphasising and repeating that sashiko stitches are large and even, and that it may take you a little while to become comfortable with this concept. Don't measure your stitches and aim for a certain number to the inch – just keep the words 'large' and 'even' in your mind. If you really must have a defined ideal measurement to match your stitches to, Fig 2 gives you an indication of the size and length of stitches which work well for sashiko.

Figure 2

Secondary patterns

Secondary patterns are great fun to experiment with once you are comfortable with the basics of stitching sashiko style. You will see from Fig 3 the effect that can be obtained where two or more lines of stitching meet or cross each other. If you are careful to space your stitches on the first line so that there is a gap at the junction, it is easier to space subsequent lines in the same way. Essentially what you are doing is suggesting the junction by leaving space rather than having the stitches pile on top of each other – Fig 4 shows the difference between leaving a gap at the junction and having stitches cross each other. If you look at the photograph, you will see that equally interesting effects can be produced on other patterns such as the chrysanthemum on page 82, where the stitches have been 'lined up' with the result that radiating circles seem to appear.

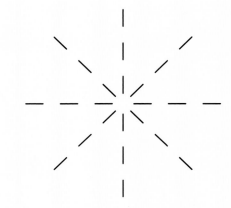

Figure 3

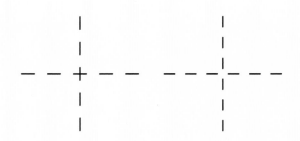

Figure 4

SASHIKO FOLD-OVER CUSHION

Sample the delights of sashiko quilting for yourself with this easy wrap-around cushion cover.

YOU WILL NEED

2 x 30-inch (77cm) squares of plain navy cotton fabric
Thread or safety pins for basting
Light-coloured fabric marker
Darning or sashiko needle
Soft white cotton thread, perle #5 or #8
Plastic or cardboard for templates
Ruler
Matching or contrasting straight tape for ties

Finished size: 27 inches (69cm) square

1　Begin by pressing both squares of fabric. Then measure and mark a line along each side of the top square approximately 1 inch (2.5cm) in from the cut edge – this will be the outer limit of your stitching.

2　Now fold the four corners of the square towards the centre and press lightly to leave a crease (Fig 5). This defines the front and back areas of the cushion. Mark lightly along the creases so that you can see these boundaries more clearly. The finished cushion will be folded as shown in Fig 6. Fig 7 shows the unfolded cushion square with the pattern areas marked out.

3　Decide how you will place the patterns shown on page 82. You may want to change the arrangement used in Fig 8. When you have settled on the layout

Figure 7

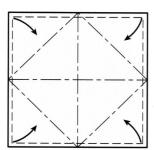

Figure 5

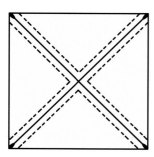

Figure 6

Figure 8

81

you want, mark the fabric using the templates and ruler as necessary. If you use chalk or a water-soluble marker, you can easily erase the markings and start again if you change your mind at the last minute.

4   Stitch or pin-baste the two squares of fabric together. Then put the templates, ruler, fabric marker, thread and a small pair of scissors into a plastic bag and you are ready to take your cushion project anywhere and stitch on the move if the opportunity arises.

5   If you plan to try creating secondary patterns in your work, it is a good idea to build up a little familiarity with the technique and how your stitches look before tackling any areas where secondary patterns could be developed. This can be done by stitching the lines which define and divide the design areas first and also any easy straight line patterns such as those in two of the corner triangles.

6   Once you have finished stitching the design, hem the edges. Use the 'outer limit' line you marked initially as a guide to work a line of running stitch around all four sides of the square. Fold both sets of raw edges to the inside and baste or pin them in place. Fold the corners of the finished sashiko square over a cushion covered with plain contrasting fabric, and tie the cords or tapes in place. Insert a length of cord or tape between the layers at each of the four corners and work another line of running stitch all around the edge just a few threads in from the folded edge. This is exactly the same as the 'sides to middle' finish for traditional quilting described on page 17. As you will be stitching through four layers of fabric, you may find you have to take one stitch at a time, rather than loading two or more stitches onto your needle.

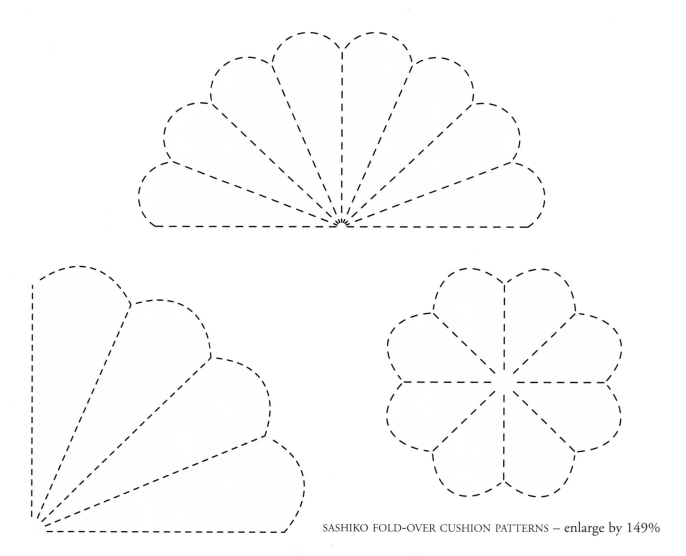

SASHIKO FOLD-OVER CUSHION PATTERNS – enlarge by 149%

Opposite: Sashiko cushion and table runner

SASHIKO FOLD-OVER
CUSHION PATTERNS —
enlarge by 149%

SASHIKO TABLE RUNNER

This table runner could easily be made into a decorative wallhanging by adding narrow sleeves (see page 21) on the reverse of the two short edges so that bamboo canes could be slipped through. There was no pre-planning for this project – it was made 'just for fun' with divisions marked out in almost haphazard fashion and then filled with different patterns as fancy dictated, with no consideration for balance, contrast or proportion. With hindsight, it would have been better to take a little more time over the planning, as you are sure to do, but the stitching was great fun nonetheless.

YOU WILL NEED

2 pieces of plain dark fabric 52 x 22 inches (133 x 56cm). Either cut these separately or fold a 1½-yard (1.5m) length of 44-inch (107cm) wide fabric in half lengthways.
Pins and thread for basting
Darning or sashiko needle
White thread, cotton perle #5 or #8
Light-coloured fabric marker
Ruler
Template material

Finished size: 48 x 20 inches (122 x 51cm)

1   Trace the patterns on pages 86–87 and decide which of them you want to include in your sashiko sampler. Set aside some time to experiment with making patterns for yourself looking at variations of scale and different combinations.

2   Pre-wash and press the fabrics before beginning to mark out the design. Mark a line a generous distance, say 1 inch (2.5cm), in from each raw edge to define the overall design area. Divide this area into smaller sections of different sizes as suggested in Fig 9 to give the framework for your sampler, then mark your chosen patterns in the various sections using templates and ruler as appropriate. It is not absolutely necessary to mark

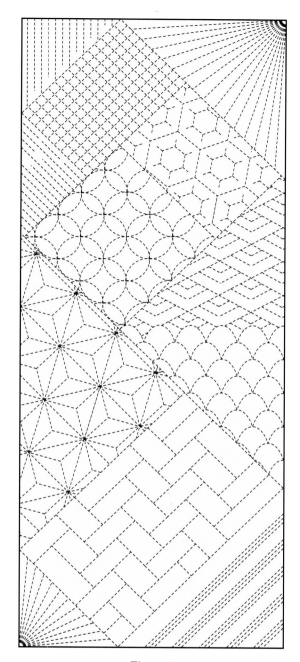

Figure 9

everything out before you begin; many light-coloured markers have an endearing habit of removing themselves from the fabric as it is handled and scrunched during stitching, so you may prefer to baste first and then mark and stitch one section at a time.

3   Stitch all the framework lines before going on to work the smaller individual sections of pattern. When you have completed all the sections, you can make tassels by knotting together any lengths of thread that were left before turning in the raw edges as described and securing them with a line of running stitch through all the thicknesses.

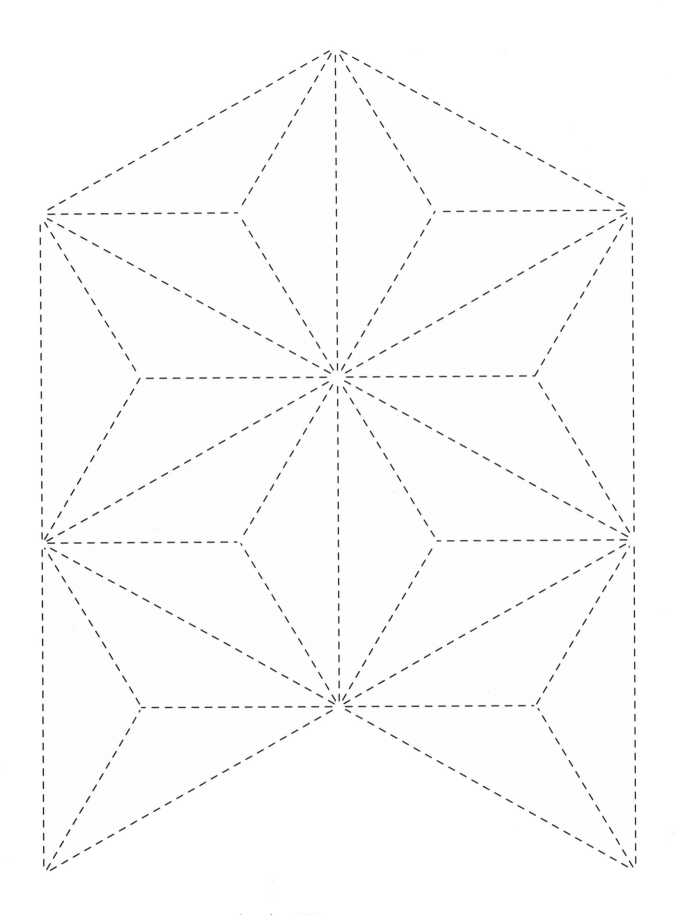

SASHIKO TABLE RUNNER PATTERNS – enlarge by 125%

SASHIKO TABLE RUNNER FULL-SIZE PATTERNS

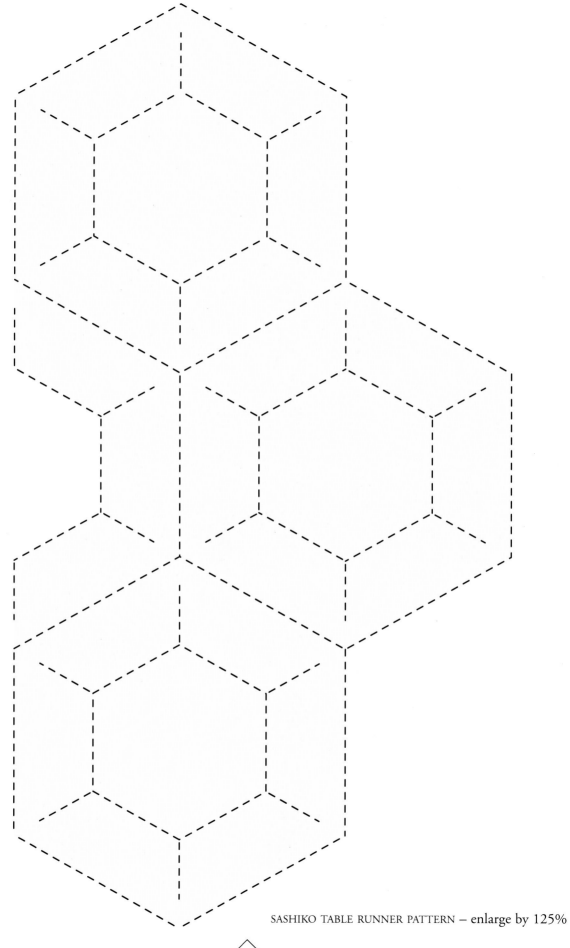

SASHIKO TABLE RUNNER PATTERN – enlarge by 125%

INDIAN QUILTING OR KANTHA WORK

The kantha quilting tradition of India has been a source of inspiration for many quilters. Constructed from two or more layers of soft cotton fabric, these stitched cloths were, and still are, both decorative and functional. The fabric is most usually white or neutral in colour and the running stitches, worked in coloured threads, which hold the layers together give both pattern and texture to the finished piece. Kanthas can be any size, from bedcover to handkerchief, simple to ornate.

The subtle textures produced from densely worked stitching through several layers of soft fine cotton fabric give kantha work its particular and unique appeal and make it so attractive and satisfying to work. The overall effect is less stark and more colourful than sashiko, which traditionally has strong contrasts of indigo fabric and coarse white thread. Both techniques focus attention on the spaces between the stitches as a means of building up secondary patterns and texture to great effect. By changing the length of the basic running stitch, it is easy to build up patterns and motifs which then become part of the larger overall design (Figs 10 and 11).

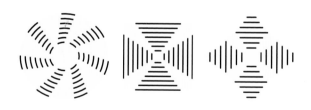

Figure 10

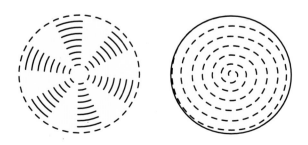

Figure 11

Fabrics

Being incorporated into a kantha was often the final destiny of fabric which had seen much previous wear and tear as clothing or household linen, and this layering of thin, worn fabrics together with an overall density and closeness of stitching gives traditional kanthas their distinctively soft 'handle'. Traditionally the threads used for stitching were also 'pre-used', perhaps being unravelled from colourful sari cloth. Like patchwork, kantha making in its original form was a salvage craft and the final results also often belied its humble origins.

If you want to work with all-new fabrics to create your own kantha, choose a very lightweight muslin or lawn and prewash it for maximum softness. You might like to experiment on a small scale with some 'pre-used' fabric of your own – elderly handkerchiefs are an ideal weight and can be purloined from the clean washing basket without anyone being any the wiser. It would perhaps be too sweeping to say that virtually any type of fine or medium thread can be used, but you do have a very wide choice, ranging from ordinary sewing thread to stranded embroidery floss, with no thread being more 'correct' than another. The same freedom of choice extends to the type of needle. Whatever type feels comfortable and allows you to stitch easily through the fabric layers is fine. As for any other quilting, the fabric layers will need to be basted together to prevent them from shifting during the stitching process (stitch basting is probably preferable to safety pins), and the main elements of the design should be marked on the top layer before you begin to baste. Once this very basic preparation is done, you are ready to settle back and enjoy stitching.

Stitching kantha

The stitch itself is a running stitch and there are no absolutes as to the size and appearance of the stitch – what bliss! The fascination and enjoyment of this type of quilting is the freedom to experiment and create all sorts of intriguing patterns and effects depending on how the stitches are aligned.

One of the distinguishing features of kantha work is that both the main shapes and the background are filled with stitch, unlike sashiko and traditional Western quilting, where the stitch outlines the main shapes and fills in the background. You can use the same colour thread for both outline and infill, or you could use dark thread for the outline and a different shade for the infill. When it comes to stitching the background, you can use a matching or a contrasting thread depending on the effect you want. Matching

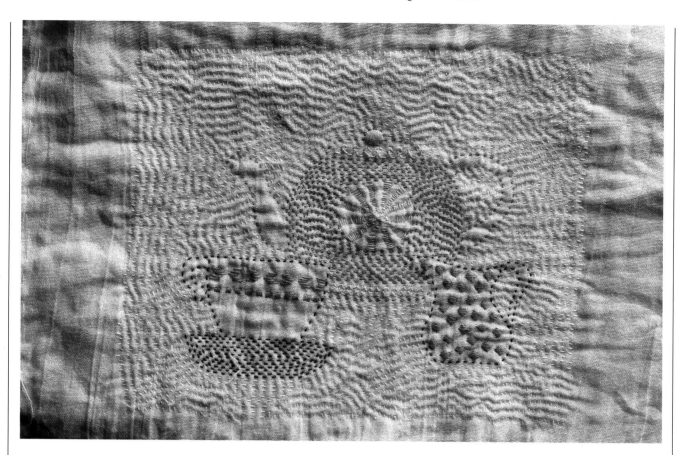

English and Indian traditions meet in this charming Kantha tea pot and "cuppa" designed and stitched by Lynne Williams.

thread will blend into the texture, whereas a contrasting thread will give an impression of speckling. For large areas of infilling try subdividing into smaller areas which will give character and liveliness to the finished work (Fig 12) rather than just repeating or echoing the outer line of the shape.

On a strictly practical note, you can start and finish threads by leaving a knot on the reverse side and perhaps taking one or two tiny back stitches through the last couple of layers of cloth. Kanthas have a 'right' and a 'wrong' side, unlike traditional quilting which should be reversible. You may prefer to hide starting and finishing knots in the layers in much the same way as you would for quilting – it's a matter of what you feel is best and works well for you.

Everyday items – coffee pots, sewing machine, fruit, vegetables, flowers, gardening tools – make charming subjects suitable for kantha designs The kantha piece by Lynne Williams shown here depicts that very English ceremony – tea. You could start your own kantha sampler and include lots of your favourites.

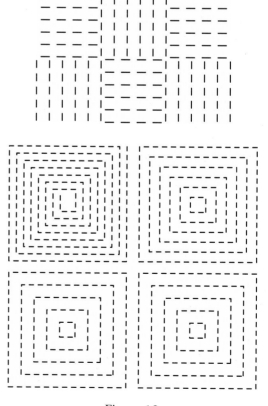

Figure 12

CAT CUSHION

This charming cat cushion designed and stitched by Sue Longhurst is a perfect project to try kantha work for yourself. Measuring 14 inches (35cm) square, it is a manageable size to carry around with you so that you can stitch whenever you have a few spare moments.

YOU WILL NEED

3 x 16-inch (40cm) squares of very lightweight cotton fabric
Selection of coloured cotton threads
Needle
Fabric marker

Finished size: 14 inches (36cm) square

These requirements are for the front of the cushion only – you will need a second 16-inch (40cm) square to form the back. This could be a heavier-weight cotton or furnishing fabric, or even one of those unfinished patchwork blocks you have hidden away somewhere.

1   Pre-wash and press the fabrics. Trace one or both of the cat shapes opposite and use the tracing to make templates.

2   Position the template on the top layer of fabric and trace around it using your preferred marker, moving the template and retracing around it as many times as necessary to give you the arrangement you want – remember you can flip the template over from time to time so that the cats don't all face the same way.

3   Once the cat shapes are marked on the top fabric, place it on the other layers and baste them all together.

4   Now start stitching. One sequence which works well is to outline all the cat shapes first and then fill them in before working the background. Have fun trying to make each cat a little different from the others in some way, either with colour of threads or how the infill is worked (Fig 13).

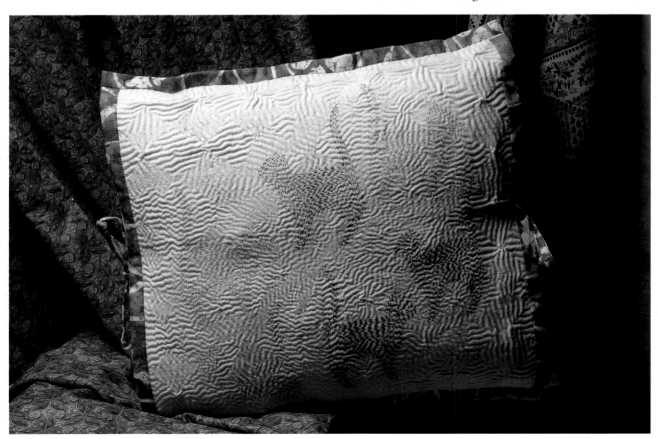

Delightful kantha cat cushion designed and stitched by Sue Longhurst.

CAT CUSHION FULL SIZE PATTERNS

Just remember to keep the overall density of stitching broadly the same if you can.

Sue finished the cushion front and back with binding, which allowed her to incorporate the ties into the binding seams.

Big stitch quilting

American quilter Jo Walters has done much to promote this increasingly popular technique, which was used on many utility quilts in the past, especially in the African–American tradition, and now offers an interesting and most effective adjunct to mainstream quilting. Large, even running stitches are worked through the three quilt layers with a soft thick thread such as perle cotton in a toning or even contrasting colour and an appropriately sized needle. As with kantha quilting, the secret of success lies in having an even density of stitching, and many of the linear sashiko patterns, which originally inspired Jo, translate very well into this technique. Although no specific project is given to illustrate this technique, you might like to experiment with it for yourself.

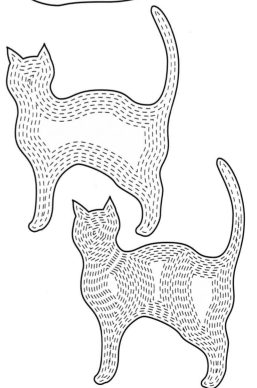

Figure 13

CHAPTER SIX

Quilting with Patchwork and Appliqué

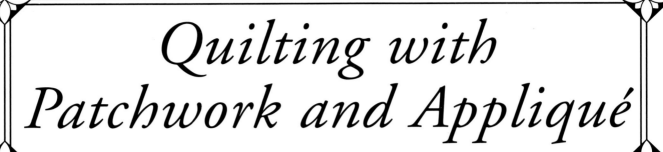

The majority of stitchers seem to discover quilting after acquiring some patchwork and/or appliqué skills. Quilting is no longer seen as a separate 'discipline' and since the beginning of the revival of interest in these traditional needlearts, the word 'patchworkquilt' has been frequently heard and used. Quilting, by the very nature of the texture it produces, adds considerably to the overall effect of both patchwork and appliqué. During the last ten years there has been a tremendous increase in the number of items quilted by machine as the pressures on free or sewing time increase and quilters are ever more eager to finish projects quickly so they can go on to the next. The happy outcome is that more and more machine quilting is being done and, most importantly, being done well. Something similar has happened with handquilting too. Instead of working just basic outline quilting around the lines of the piecing or appliqué, which used to be the norm, many of today's quilters are focusing their attention and efforts on elaborate close quilting which truly adds a third dimension to their work. Both the amount and quality of quilting, done either by hand or machine, are an increasingly important part of pieced or appliqué quilts.

There is no magic formula for deciding what quilting treatment will work best on a particular project. If there were, the majority of quilts would be very boring and predictable indeed. Rather, it is the endless possibilities which are so fascinating – look at the simple 9-patch block in Fig 1 and see how it is changed by different, but simple, quilting, none of which require special patterns and all easy to mark or judge 'by eye'. Now look at Fig 2, which shows five stylised shapes, and again you will see how changing the additional quilting lines alters their appearance. Bear in mind that any one of these suggestions will look more subtle and yet more dramatic when worked 'in the cloth' rather than as black lines on a white background.

Figure 2

Quilting with patchwork

Outline quilting is probably best defined as stitching around the main or dominant shapes of patchwork at a consistent distance from the seams. This distance is determined by your preference and could be anything from right against the seams to ¼ inch (5mm) away from them. If you quilt right against the seams you will have to contend with stitching through seam

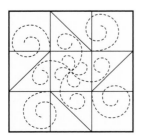 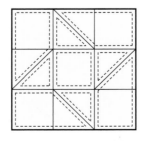

Figure 1

Opposite: Subtly different background quilting on these quilts designed and stitched by Patricia Cox.

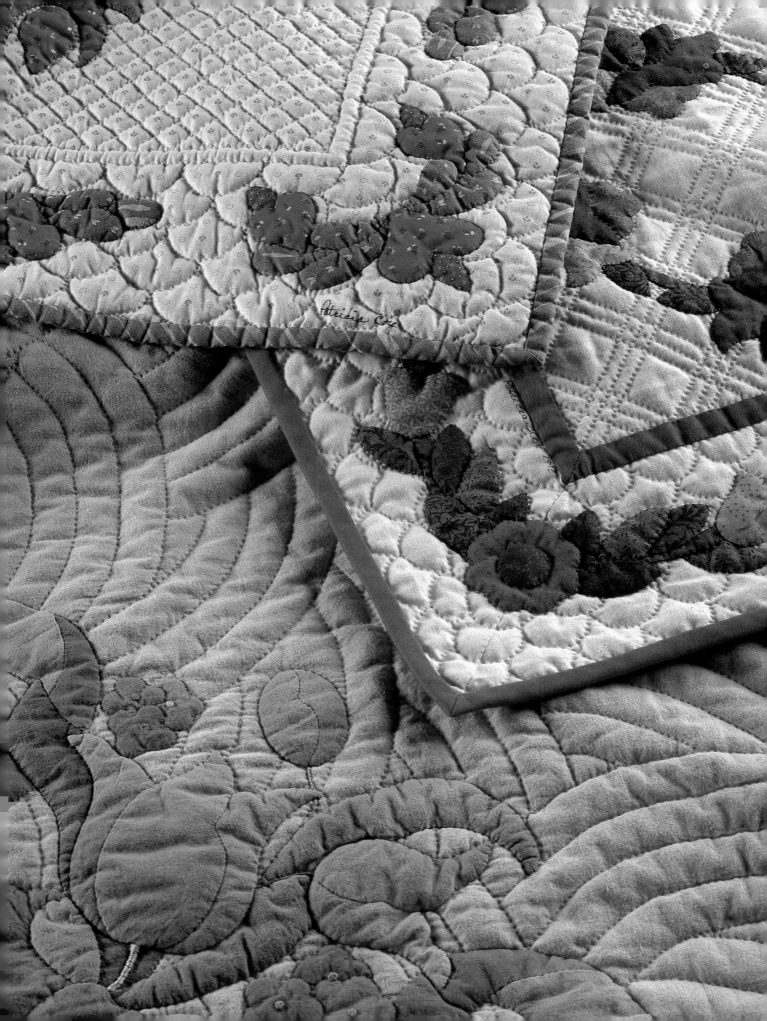

allowances, which for hand quilting can be slow and also affects the evenness of your stitches. There will be times when you will be stitching through more than one set of seam allowances. Don't worry if you guiltily resort to stab stitching in an effort just to get the needle through the layers. This is perfectly acceptable and everyone does it from time to time. Machine quilting with a walking foot over seam allowances can be far less traumatic. Outline quilting ¼ inch (5mm) away from the seams will lessen or virtually eliminate the problems of stitching through additional layers, by hand or machine. When deciding on the distance you want to use for a particular project, consider that a line of quilting has the effect of raising up the fabric to either side of it. If it is important to create sharp definition around your main patchwork shapes, this will be easier to achieve by quilting close to the seams.

In the majority of cases, outline quilting of some sort is necessary to define the main elements of the design, whether it is pieced or appliquéd –think of it as a skeleton on which you can build further with more quilting. If however you really don't want to do outline quilting, and anyway you can't seem to come up with ideas for quilting a particular piece, another option exists that may also be easier (and faster). 'Old time' quilters often used allover designs which ignored all pieced or appliquéd shapes and were, as the description suggests, worked over the whole quilt. These designs were usually very simple, relatively quick to work and gave a pleasing, evenly balanced texture with added cohesion (Fig 3). Often the use of quilting motifs in the patchwork or appliqué spaces can give a spotty look to the finished pieces. An overall pattern pulls everything together, especially in scrap quilts, without detracting from the fabrics, and is an increasingly popular approach, particularly where a 'country' look is wanted.

The main object of quilting for both patchwork and appliqué is to have an even balance and spread of quilting across the whole top and for the quilting to enhance and emphasise specific areas. The original need for close and evenly spread quilting was to hold the batting (either cotton or wool) in position without undue shifting or bunching. The advent of polyester battings, which move less, meant that less quilting was required, and for several years minimal, or absolutely basic, quilting ruled, with most of the individual quilter's attention focused on the piecing, colour and shapes. We are now seeing a return to more elaborate and close quilting done both by hand and machine, but there is a feeling of wanting to reserve hand quilting for special projects only. Perhaps we feel we are running out of time.

A useful 'rule of thumb' for selecting background quilting patterns is that curved lines will contrast well with straight seams, straight lines with curved edges. It is very easy to add a feeling of movement to any pieced project by using a few simple curved lines instead of the straight lines of outline quilting (see Fig 1, page 94). This rule of thumb can be seen frequently on appliqué quilts where crosshatching or grids of varying complexity are used to fill in the background, contrasting with the irregular and curved shapes of appliqué shapes/design.

Motifs should fill as much of the available space as possible (Fig 4). The style of the motif(s) can contrast with or reflect shapes which have already been used, for example a feather wreath or circular pattern within the 'blank' square next to a 9-patch block, or crosshatching to echo the straight lines of a pieced pattern.

Backgrounds are an underrated part of quilting to enhance patchwork and appliqué, and few of them

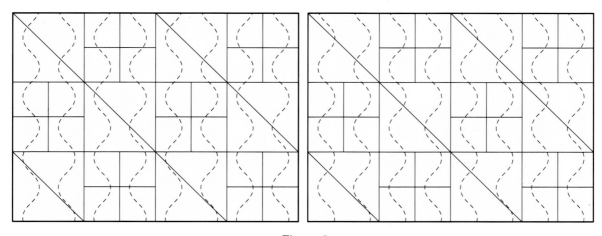

Figure 3

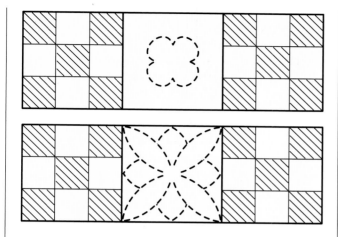

Figure 4

have yet been over-used. From the straightforward crosshatch to the gentle curves of clamshell, there is a wide range of possibilities, all simple enough to mark and stitch and all adding considerably to the overall impact of a quilt. Appliqué, with its freer non-geometric lines and open spaces, offers great scope for thoughtful and well-considered background quilting. Appliqué experts such as American quilter Patricia Cox are constantly experimenting with backgrounds that enhance the main designs and are also just that little bit different from the almost traditional choice of crosshatching. Three of Patricia's many quilts are shown on page 95. One of the reasons for choosing and using crosshatching is that the lines will usually fall on the bias of the fabric, which is the easiest direction in which to hand stitch.

Appliqué in particular benefits from the judicious use of a double line around the outer edges of the shapes to give a clear yet subtle definition. Quilt the first line very close to the edge of the appliqué and a second a scant ¼ inch (5mm) outside it – see the photograph of the tulip cushion on page 119. The same principle applies to wholecloth quilting, particularly when the project is large in scale – a double line worked around the outside of the main pattern shapes gives extra clarity.

Meander quilting (see page 66) is immensely popular for machine-worked backgrounds on both pieced and appliqué quilts, so much so that one quilting judge was recently heard to remark that she didn't care if she never saw any again. Because it is easy to do and nearly always looks good, it does seem to be in danger of being over-used. Once you have sufficient confidence, why not try something a fraction more adventurous and not a great deal more demanding? The sketches in Fig 5 may give you some ideas to try out.

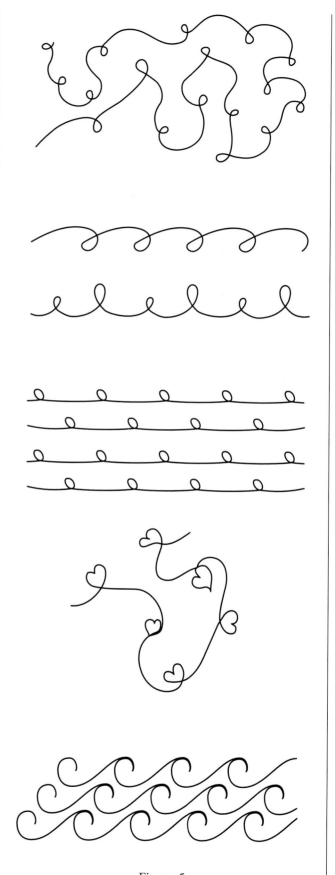

Figure 5

Patchwork principles

Patchwork or piecing can be as simple or complex as you wish it to be and is endlessly fascinating in its own right. The piecing of the projects in this book has been deliberately kept simple. Here are some of the basic guidelines:

Always use sharp scissors for cutting fabric and keep a second pair for cutting paper, batting, template plastic, etc. Label both pairs so you remember which is which and don't let them out of your sight.

Measure, mark and cut as accurately as you can, whether it be templates or fabric.

Mark fabrics on the wrong side with as fine a line as possible. For hand piecing you will be marking the stitching line, for machine piecing you mark the cutting line only.

For hand piecing you will mark only the sewing line and cut an additional seam allowance 'by eye'.

For machine piecing you will mark the cutting line and stitch all the required pieces together in sequence using a consistent seam allowance (usually ¼ inch/ 5mm).

For hand piecing use a small running stitch which incorporates a backstitch from time to time. Begin and end with a combination of knot and backstitches.

For machine piecing set the stitch length for approximately 12 stitches per inch. Stitch from raw edge to raw edge rather than start and finish each seam. One tip which improved my machine piecing

accuracy enormously is to spray-starch and press all fabrics before marking and cutting, and then lightly spray-starch each pair of patches before pressing the seam first flat and then to the darker side. The starch adds enough temporary weight and firmness to the pieces to make you feel confident about stitching accurately and consistently – try it for yourself.

Chain piecing

If you need to piece a number of similar units, chain piecing speeds up the process by eliminating the need to stop and start each time. Stitch from raw edge to raw edge on the first pair of patches and gently feed the next pair towards the foot with the machine still running. Snip the paired patches apart and press the seam first flat and then to one side before going on to the next stage.

Thread

A standard cotton sewing thread in a neutral colour such as cream or pale grey works well for most projects, whether you work by hand or by machine.

For both hand and machine piecing it is standard practice to press seams to one side – usually toward the darker colour to help prevent the seam allowance from showing through on the right side of the work.

The selection of projects which follows is aimed at giving you more practice with both hand and machine quilting in the form of outlining, motifs and backgrounds.

SPINNING STAR CUSHION

Straight line or meander quilting

This simple Spinning Star patchwork cushion is an ideal project for practising straight-line machine quilting using a walking foot, although you might like to make two identical cushions and use straight line quilting in the background spaces of one and free scribble quilting for the other.

YOU WILL NEED

Scraps or fat quarters of three different fabrics for the pieced block
22-inch (55cm) square of fabric for cushion back
22-inch (55cm) square of backing fabric
22-inch (55cm) square of lightweight needlepunched batting
Fat quarter of fabric for border (optional)
Sewing thread to match background fabric or invisible thread for quilting
Sewing thread for piecing
Pins
Template material and fabric scissors
Fine-line fabric marker

Finished size: 20 inches (51cm) square including borders

1   Trace and make templates (page 100).
2   Mark around the templates onto the wrong side of the fabrics and cut out 1 square A for the centre of the star, 4 squares A from the background fabric and 8 triangles B, 4 from the background fabric and 4 from the main or star fabric.
3   Following the sequence in Figs 6, 7, 8 and 9; assemble the Spinning Star block, progressing from the triangles-into-squares units into strips and finally the complete block. Press each set of seams as you go.
4   Measure, mark and cut fabric strips of desired width for the borders. For the cushion on the right,

Figure 6

Figure 7

Figure 8

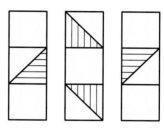

Figure 9

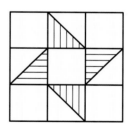

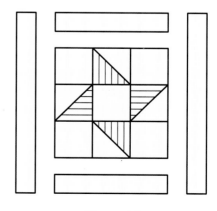

Figure 10

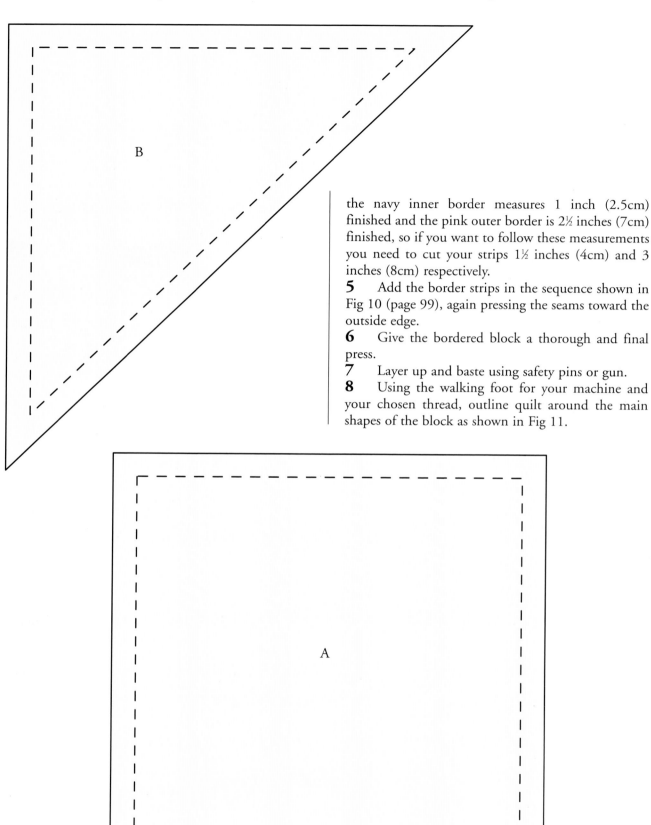

the navy inner border measures 1 inch (2.5cm) finished and the pink outer border is 2½ inches (7cm) finished, so if you want to follow these measurements you need to cut your strips 1½ inches (4cm) and 3 inches (8cm) respectively.

5 Add the border strips in the sequence shown in Fig 10 (page 99), again pressing the seams toward the outside edge.

6 Give the bordered block a thorough and final press.

7 Layer up and baste using safety pins or gun.

8 Using the walking foot for your machine and your chosen thread, outline quilt around the main shapes of the block as shown in Fig 11.

SPINNING STAR CUSHION FULL SIZE TEMPLATES

Easy patchwork/piecing and simple machine quilting on this pair of cushions.

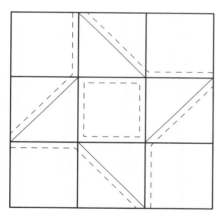

Figure 11

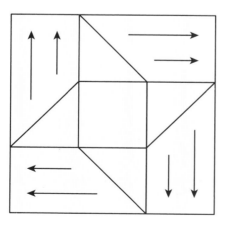

Figure 12

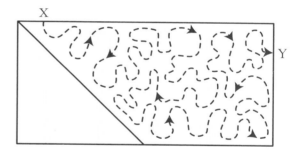

Figure 13

9   Depending on your preference you can fill in the background space with straight lines as shown in Fig 12 or use meander quilting (Fig 13).

If you choose the straight line option, it is best to keep all the lines within one section running in the same direction to give a good crisp appearance. For meander quilting, switch from the walking to the darning foot for your machine and drop or cover the feed dogs (see page 66). A suggested starting point and stitching route for each section is given in Fig 13.

You might also consider adding quilting within the main pattern shapes. Then, using the walking foot, quilt on or close to the two sets of border seams.

10   Finally, trim away any excess batting and backing flush with top, and the quilted Spinning Star is ready to be made up into a cushion using your preferred method.

GEORGIAN GEESE

This small quilt or wallhanging is simple both to piece and to quilt. You could choose your fabrics from one colour family, as in this example, or use scraps of many colours for a completely different look.

YOU WILL NEED

1 fat quarter of each of 7 different fabrics (this is an exceptionally generous allowance and will leave you enough to make another similar quilt) or scraps
½ yard (0.5m) of background fabric
1 yard (1m) of fabric for the border and binding
1 ¼ yards (1 generous metre) of fabric for the back of the quilt
40-inch (101cm) square of lightweight needlepunched batting
Safety pins or basting gun
Invisible thread or threads to match background and border fabrics
Template material
Fabric marker
Fabric scissors
Thread for piecing

Finished size: 34 inches (87cm) square

1   Trace and make templates from page 106–107.
2   Mark around the templates onto the wrong side of the fabric and cut them out.
For the centre star cut:
  1 square of main fabric, template C.
  4 squares of background fabric, template D.
  8 triangles of main fabric, template A.
  4 triangles of background fabric, template B.
For the pieced border, cut:
  16 triangles of assorted fabrics, template B.
  48 triangles of background fabric, template A.
  8 triangles of main fabric, template A.
Piece together following the sequence shown in Figs 14, 15 and 16. Assemble all the triangle or 'geese' units first. Using chain piecing to add a small triangle to the same side of all the large triangles will speed

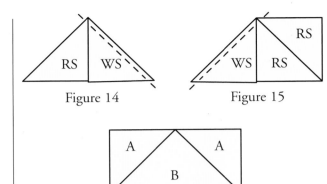

Figure 14   Figure 15

Figure 16

things up a little. Press all the seams towards the background and then repeat the chain piecing sequence and pressing with the second small triangles.
3   Once all the triangle units are pieced and pressed, join them into four strips of four units (Fig 17).

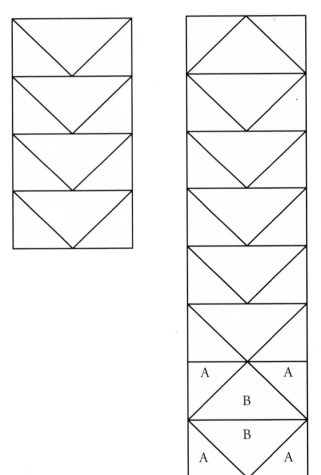

Figure 17

Small quilt/wallhanging with easy piecing and outline machine quilting, quilted by Sally Radway. Fabrics courtesy of Rose & Hubble Ltd.

4 Assemble and press the strips for the centre star (Fig 18) and make it up. Add the square units to two

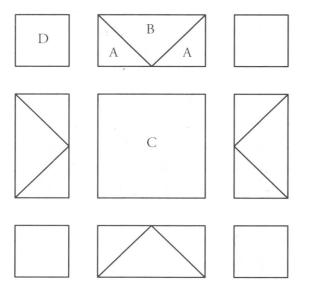

Figure 18

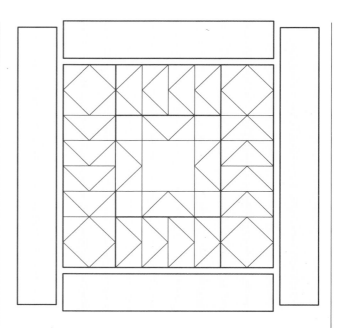

Figure 20

of the four strips for the inner border (Fig 19) and stitch the remaining two strips to the top and bottom of the centre block. Add the two longer strips to the sides of the centre block, and then press everything again.

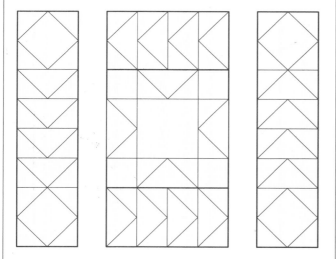

Figure 19

5 Measure, mark and cut four strips for outer border and add these in the sequence shown in Fig 20. Give the completed top a final press.

6 Layer up and baste in the usual way with either safety pins or gun and tags.

7 Begin quilting in the centre of the piece, using the left-hand edge of the walking foot to keep a

The crisp definition of outline quilting works well with simple geometric shapes.

consistent distance away from the seams. You can use invisible monofilament or matching thread. Remember to start with a short stitch length, increasing to your standard stitch length and decreasing as you finish, then take the starting and finishing threads through to reverse or wrong side of the work to tie off. This small quilt will give you plenty of practice in outline quilting. Each of the smaller triangles forming the outer edge is outlined (Fig 21), so you will be expert at increasing and decreasing stitch length by the time you have finished! A different straight line quilting treatment is suggested in Fig 22, page 106.

Why not also try your hand (or machine) at some simple lines in the border and centre square?

8   When you have completed all the quilting, trim away any excess fabric so that the edges are flush with the top. Finally, secure the threads as necessary and bind to finish (see page 17).

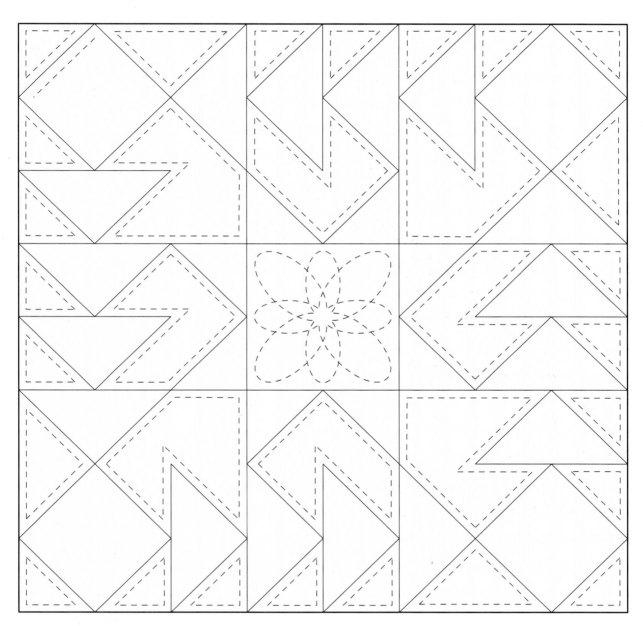

Figure 21

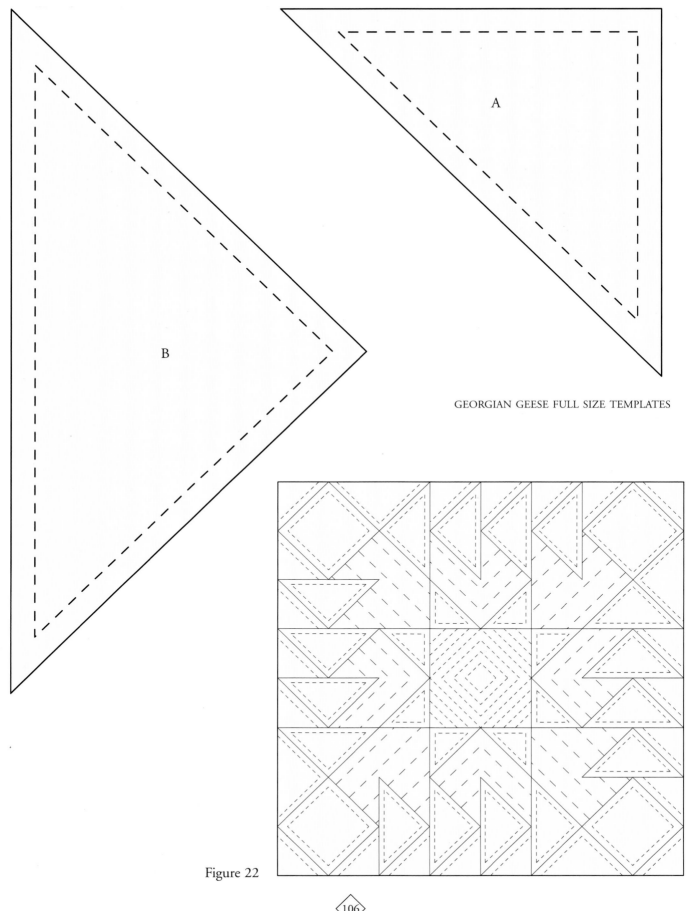

A

GEORGIAN GEESE FULL SIZE TEMPLATES

B

Figure 22

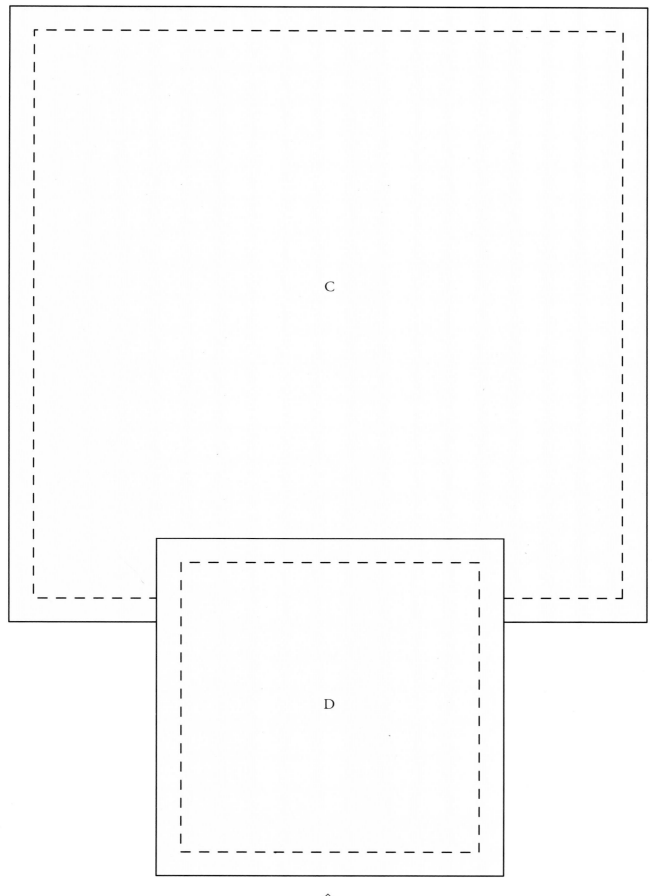

C

D

PINK AND WHITE PATCHWORK QUILT

The pieced blocks of this single-bed quilt were made using a quick piecing technique similar to that used in the Christmas 9-patch (page 114), which meant that this quilt top was constructed in less than two days. Of course, the hand quilting took just a fraction longer than this to complete! There is plenty of scope for quilting on this style of quilt where blank or plain blocks are part of the overall design. Outline quilting and a feathered square pattern feature on this quilt, although you are free to use any other pattern and ideas you may have.

YOU WILL NEED

6 fat quarters in toning prints for the pieced blocks
1 yard (1m) of contrasting fabric for the spacer blocks
2 yards (2m) of fabric for the border and binding. This could be one of the fabrics used in the pieced blocks.
3 yards (2.75m) fabric for the quilt backing
Pre-cut single-bed size pack of 2-ounce batting
Ruler, fabric marker and scissors or rotary cutter, ruler and mat
Thread for piecing
Threads to tone with or match spacer blocks and possibly main colour of pieced blocks
Basting thread
Quilting hoop or frame
Quilting needles
Fabric marker
Tracing paper

Finished size: 49 x 79 inches (124 x 200cm)

1 Each pieced block is made from 16 small squares in a non-repeating arrangement. A quick and easy way of making the 12 blocks for this quilt is to cut strips 2⅞ inches (7.5cm) wide from each of your six chosen fabrics and seam these strips together into four differently arranged bands of four. The sequence of the stripped bands could be 1234, 2345, 3456 and 4561 – the idea is that when the block is complete, the arrangement of the fabrics appears to be totally random (Fig 23). Use the standard ¼ inch (5mm) seam allowance, pressing seams all in one direction.

2 Measure, mark and cut the pieced bands apart into 2⅞ inch (7.5cm) slices (Fig 24).

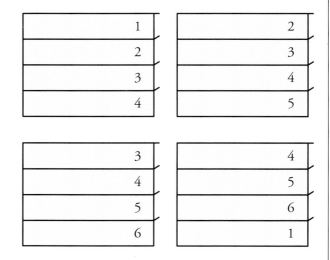

Figure 23

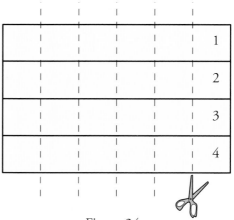

Figure 24

Opposite: This fresh pink and white quilt is fast to piece, but will take a little longer to hand quilt.

1
2
3
4

2
3
4
5

3
4
5
6

4
5
6
1

Figure 25

1	2	3	4
2	3	4	5
3	4	5	6
4	5	6	1

Figure 26

9½ in
(24cm)

13¼ in
(33.5cm)

A

9½ in
(24cm)

7 in
(17.5cm)

9½ in
(24cm)

B

7 in
(17.5cm)

Figure 27

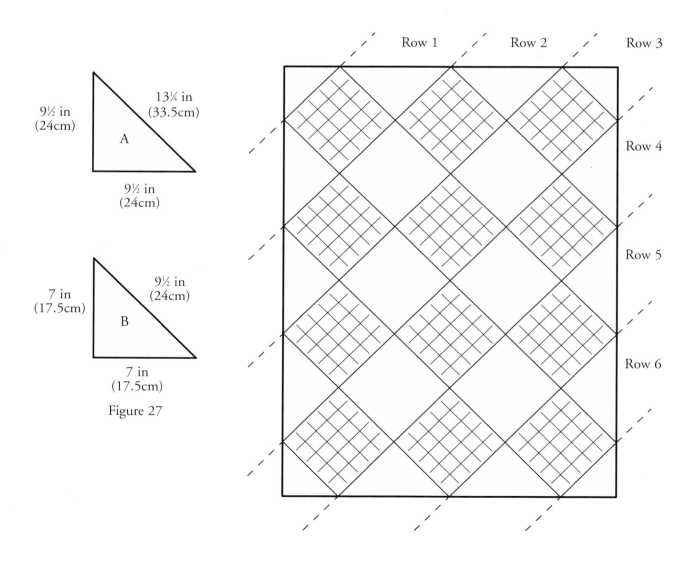

Figure 28

3   Now you can either select random slices and join them into pairs and then into sets of four (Fig 25) or use one of each set of slices for each block, similarly joining them first into pairs and then sets of four. The goal is to have a total of 12 blocks in which no two adjacent rows are identical (Fig 26).

4   Once the blocks are made and pressed, measure, mark and cut out from the contrasting fabric six spacer blocks 10 inches (25.5cm) square (this measurement includes a ¼ inch (5mm) seam allowance).

Also from the contrasting background fabric measure, mark and cut out 10 larger triangles (A) and 4 corner triangles (B) – see Fig 27 for measurements.

5   Following the sequence shown in Fig 28, join the pieced and spacer blocks together into diagonal rows and then join the rows together. If you press the seams to one side and in opposing directions row by row, it will be easier to match up the seams as the rows are joined to complete the quilt top.

6   On the original quilt the borders were made deeper at the top and bottom, narrower at the sides. This was ostensibly to make the finished quilt a better fit on the bed it was intended for, but to be truthful, had rather more to do with the amount of border fabric on hand at the time. You have the choice of following this precedent or adding borders of equal width to all four sides. The side borders on this quilt are 4½ inches (11.5cm) – this is the cutting measurement, so the border finishes at 4 inches (11cm), and the top and lower borders are 8½ inches (21cm) –

Figure 29

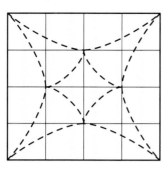

Figure 30

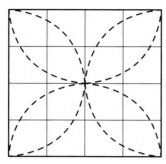

Figure 31

again, this is the cutting measurement, giving an 8-inch (20cm) finished depth. Decide whether you want equal or unequal borders and cut strips from your border fabric accordingly – the yardage given allows for four borders of 10 inches (25.5cm) cut width so that you can choose. Add the borders to the quilt top in the sequence shown in Fig 29, page 111.

7 Give the completed top a final press before marking the quilting patterns.

8 Trace and complete the quarter pattern opposite, which can either be made into a template to mark around directly onto the fabric, or if you have chosen a pale fabric for the spacer squares, you could trace the design through (see page 10). Remember to test your marker first.

9 Seam together and press your backing fabric as necessary, lay out the backing, batting and quilt top in the usual sequence, and baste.

10 Outline quilting is a popular choice for pieced quilts – it holds the layers together, emphasises the shapes and requires very little thought or planning. But it does mean that you will be stitching through seam allowances some of the time. For the places

where several seam allowances come together, make those few stitches any way you can – in other words, if you have to stab stitch sometimes, so be it. Two alternative quilting suggestions for the pieced blocks are shown in Figs 30 and 31.

The quilting pattern given for the plain blocks will give you another chance to practise using masking tape as a marker for the straight lines of the centre crosshatching. You may prefer to quilt the cross-hatched area first before working the surrounding feather loops and then a line of quilting close against the edge of the block. When you have finished quilting all the pieced and plain blocks, remember to add

a line of quilting just inside the border seam. Originally, no quilting was planned for the border of this quilt (an uncharacteristic omission on my part), but this deficiency will be rectified in the near future! Simple crosshatching, about 2 inches (5cm) apart, would echo the crosshatching at the centre of the feather patterns and give an attractive finish.

11   The quilt edges are finished here with a double-fold binding (see page 18), but you may prefer to use single-fold binding or one of the other finishing methods described on pages 17–19.

12   As a finishing touch you could incorporate some of the fabrics used for the top in the label for this quilt.

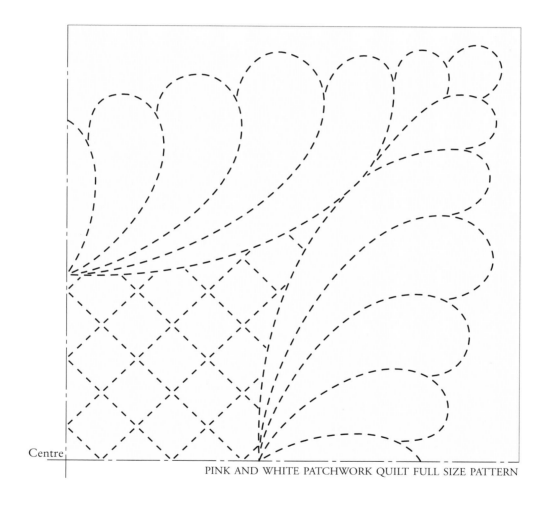

Centre

PINK AND WHITE PATCHWORK QUILT FULL SIZE PATTERN

CHRISTMAS WALLHANGING

This small quilt first began life as five 9-patch blocks made during a class demonstration on speed-piecing techniques. These were then used in a later class, along with four plain blocks, to show the basics of joining blocks together, and for good measure had some borders added. The pieced top was then pressed into service as a sample for yet another class on designing quilting for patchwork. Despite its somewhat haphazard development, this quilt is positively speedy to make and even the quilting will take less time than you think. Make it in Christmas colours, country plaids, pastels, Amish plains – just enjoy!

YOU WILL NEED

½ yard (0.5m) each of two fabrics – this is sufficient for the pieced and background blocks and the main border
¼ yard (0.25m) each of two fabrics for the narrow accent borders
¼ yard (0.25m) binding fabric
½ yard (0.5m) backing fabric
½ yard (0.5m) of standard 2-ounce batting
Thread to tone with or match background and main fabric
Basting thread
Quilting needles
Quilting hoop or frame
Fabric marker
Tracing paper and medium black marker

Finished size: 28 inches (71cm) square

1 Measure, mark and cut strips from the main and background fabrics. For Band A you will need two 2-inch (5cm) strips of the dark (or main) fabric and one 3-inch (7.5cm) strip of the light (or background) fabric. For Band B you will need two 2-inch (5cm) strips of the light (or background) fabric and one 3-inch (7.5cm) strip of the dark (or main) fabric. All strips are cut from selvage to selvage across the width of the fabric and will be 42 inches (105cm) in length. Stitch

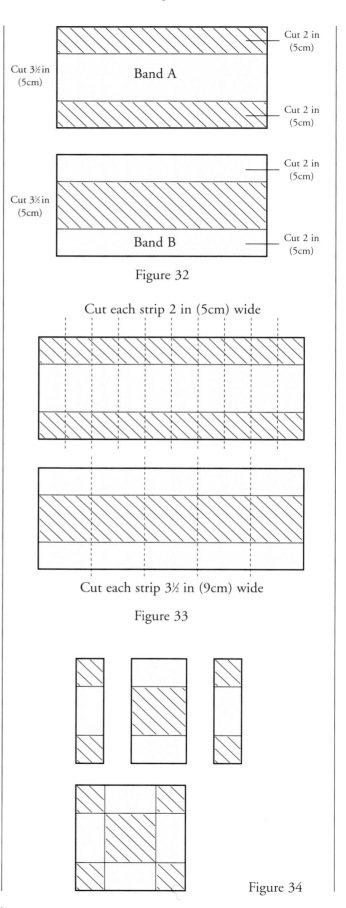

Cut 2 in (5cm)

Cut 3½ in (5cm)

Band A

Cut 2 in (5cm)

Cut 2 in (5cm)

Cut 3½ in (5cm)

Band B

Cut 2 in (5cm)

Figure 32

Cut each strip 2 in (5cm) wide

Cut each strip 3½ in (9cm) wide

Figure 33

Figure 34

the strips into bands as shown in Fig 32, pressing the seams to one side and towards the darker fabric.

2 Measure, mark and cut slices from each of the two bands shown in Fig 33 so you have ten slices from Band A measuring 2 inches (5cm) wide and five slices from Band B measuring 3½ inches (9cm) wide.

3 Join two slices from Band A to one from Band B as shown in Fig 34 to form the 9-patch blocks.

4 Measure, mark and cut out four 6½-inch (15cm) squares for the spacer/setting blocks.

5 Following the sequence shown in Fig 35, join the pieced and setting blocks together to make the top, pressing completed seams in the direction shown by the arrows.

Curves and spirals contrast well with the 9-patch blocks of this Christmas wallhanging.

6 Measure, mark and cut four strips 1½ inches (3.8cm) wide for the first accent border, four strips 1 inch (2.5cm) wide for the second accent border, and four strips 3½ inches (9cm) wide for the outer border. Add these strips to the pieced top as shown in Fig 36.

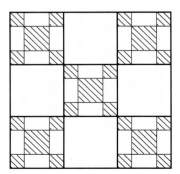

Figure 35

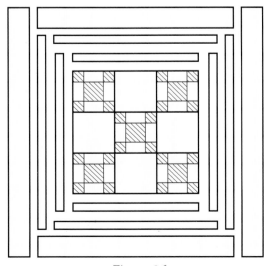

Figure 36

Press the seams on the first border towards the outside edge before adding the second accent border in the same sequence. Then press the seams to the outside again and add the final wide border strips in the same way. Press the completed top.

7 Trace the pattern below and mark it on the quilt top as indicated in Fig 37. If you have chosen a pale background fabric, you will probably be able to trace through the fabric (see page 10).

8 Baste the three layers together.

9 Quilt, working from the centre outwards. You will need to quilt close to the seams of each border in addition to working the main quilting pattern.

10 When the quilting is complete, remove the basting stitches and trim away any excess batting and backing so that the edges are flush. Finish the edges with a narrow binding or piping.

Figure 37

CHRISTMAS WALLHANGING FULL SIZE PATTERN

Centre

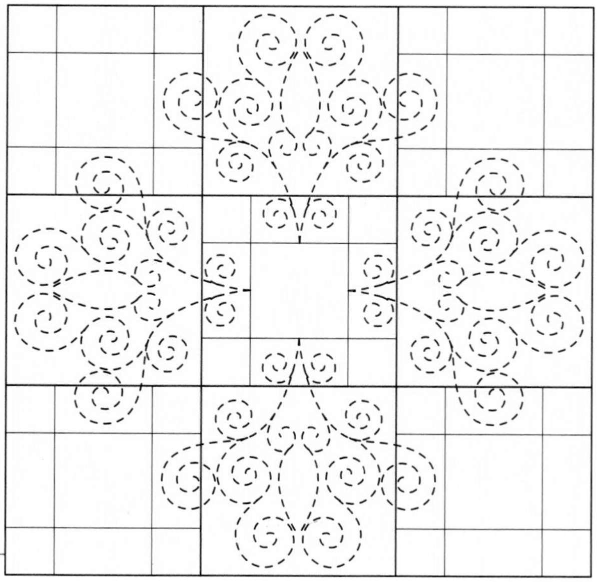

Appliqué principles

Appliqué is arguably an older needlecraft than patchwork, but along the way it seems to have acquired an undeserved reputation for being difficult and demanding. Perhaps it is easier to envisage oneself sewing the series of short straight seams which are the foundation of so much patchwork rather than the variety of curves and points of an appliqué pattern – who knows?

For traditional appliqué mark the exact shape onto the right side of the fabric and cut out allowing a scant ¼-inch (5mm) turn-under allowance all around. For deeply indented curves, clip almost to the marked line so that it is easier to turn the small allowance under.

Points and curves are not difficult. They just take a little care and practice to make them look sharp and smooth. Turn under and stitch a little at a time rather than trying to arrange a complete point or curve and then stitching it down.

It is common practice nowadays to use to match the thread to the colour of the shapes to be stitched. There are a number of different stitches which you could use, the usual choices being those which are almost invisible.

For appliqué a fine, longish needle such as a sharp is a good choice, being easy to handle and thread. The shapes themselves need to be secured into position either with basting or long fine pins before sewing – pins are a quicker, more user-friendly option.

Machine appliqué can be done from either the top or from the reverse side of the work, using a straight stitch to secure the shapes and completing the piece by outlining with a close satin stitch. No turn-under is needed.

An antique appliqué block (shown on the right) and its contemporary version have been used to make these two cushions with a folk art feel.

FOLK ART TULIP CUSHION

Quilters seem to fall into two distinct camps – those who adore appliqué and those who don't mind looking at it but would rather have their fingernails pulled out slowly rather than actually do it. Certainly no-one seems to be indifferent to it, but even if you are not a great fan of appliqué this cushion is easy to make and you can have great fun with the background quilting.

The original piece of appliqué used to make this cushion is an antique 'orphan' block. (Unfinished projects are not just the plague of today's quilter – it is still possible to find blocks and quilt tops as well as part-finished quilts in antique shops and flea markets). This particular pattern has a naive folk-art charm with the further advantage of being easy to stitch. The large simple shapes also adapt well to the increasingly popular 'cut and glue' appliqué method, in which the pieces are fused to the background fabric using lightweight fusible webbing. The alternative cushion has been made using this technique, which is ideal for those of us who are always keen to get to the quilting stage as quickly as possible. While I enjoy the process of hand appliqué, the speed of the 'cut and glue' technique has a great deal to recommend it. The start-to-finish time spent making this block was a mere twenty minutes, which included cutting the background square, cutting the shapes, and bonding them to the background as well as cutting and stitching the two borders This is surely fast enough to satisfy even the most impatient quilter!

Whichever appliqué technique you decide to use, have fun with quilting the background space. The two examples illustrated both have very simple background quilting based on straight lines which can easily be marked by using masking tape (see pages 10–11). The orphan block was quilted with triple diagonal lines, and the 'remake' was first quilted with single diagonal lines, which somehow got converted to crosshatching and finished as a starred grid virtually identical to one of the sashiko patterns on page 84.

YOU WILL NEED

16-inch (40.5cm) square of background fabric
Fabric scraps for tulip stem, leaves and flower
4 border strips 2 x 15 inches (5 x 38.5cm)
4 border strips 2 x 18 inches (5 x 49cm)
24-inch (61cm) square of 2-ounce batting
24-inch (61cm) square of backing fabric
22-inch (56cm) square of fabric for the cushion back
Plastic or cardboard for templates
Sharps needles for appliqué, betweens needles for quilting
Sewing thread to match tulip fabrics
Quilting thread
Pins
Fabric marker
Lightweight fusible webbing

Finished size: 15 inches (38cm) square without borders, 19 inches (48cm) square with borders

1   To work this block in traditional needleturn appliqué, first make a template for each of the shapes on page 120. Mark the shapes on to the right side of the fabrics and cut around the marked lines, leaving approximately ¼ inch (5mm) allowance to be turned under as the shape is stitched into position.

Figure 38

2   When all the shapes have been marked and cut, arrange them on the background fabric as shown in Fig 38 and pin them in position. Feel free to add or subtract leaves – you could build up a larger, more complex design as shown in Fig 39.

Figure 39

3 The traditional stitch for appliqué has been one which shows as little as possible on the right side of the work, and the most frequently chosen stitch is shown in Fig 40. This is the stitch used by the maker of the antique block and it is interesting that she used an ordinary white sewing thread – with a wide variety of thread colours to choose from, most of us today would choose thread to match the fabrics.

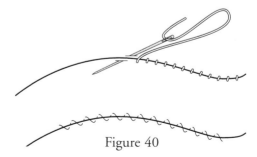

Figure 40

The folk art style of this particular design might lend itself to an alternative but equally traditional appliqué technique. The raw edges of the fabric shapes

FOLK ART TULIP CUSHION FULL SIZE TEMPLATES

are turned under and then running stitch, using a toning or even contrasting thread, is worked very close to the turned edge. This can be very quick to do and gives an additional, slightly rippled texture to the appliqué (Fig 41).

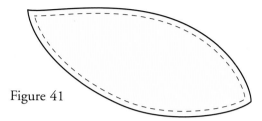

Figure 41

4 For 'cut and glue' appliqué trace and cut out each shape from fusible webbing. Iron the webbing shapes onto the wrong side of the chosen fabrics using a warm dry (no steam) iron and set aside to cool for a few moments before cutting out the fused shapes. It is easier to 'rough cut' first and then cut around the shapes exactly. Gently peel off the paper backing from each shape and arrange all the shapes in position on the background fabric. When you are satisfied with the design, fuse it to the background fabric with a warm dry iron as before. To avoid any sticky residue on your ironing surface or the iron itself, lay a sheet of baking parchment or silicone paper on the ironing surface before you begin, and use a second sheet of the same type of paper over the top of the fabric to protect the soleplate of the iron. Allow a few moments for cooling before handling the block.

If you suspect that your appliqué cushion will receive a lot of wear and tear, take a little extra time to secure the design by stitching around the shapes of the design, using a functional running stitch or perhaps a more decorative stitch such as chain stitch or blanket stitch (Fig 42) or a short machine satin stitch.

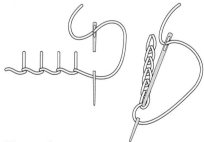

Figure 42

5 Once the design is complete, whether you have glued or stitched, add the borders in the sequence shown in Fig 43 and press the seams towards the outside edge.

Figure 43

6 Both of these examples were layered up for quilting (see page 11) without pre-marking the background quilting lines, which were worked after the main design had been outline quilted (Fig 44). Use masking tape to determine where the lines should be and as a guide to quilt along (see pages 10–11). Notice that the background quilting on the plaid tulip is the same as one of the sashiko patterns – you could use one of the other patterns if you wish.

7 Finally, make up the quilted block into a cushion using your preferred method.

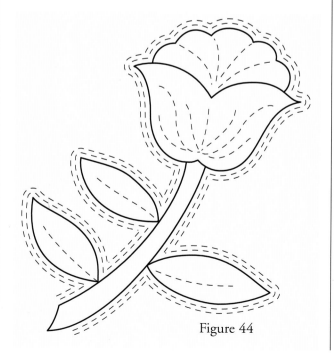

Figure 44

CHAPTER SEVEN

From the Antique

Not everyone feels creative all of the time, but we all like to add our own special touches to whatever projects we undertake. A visit to a quilt show allows us to see many exciting and different types of quilt ranging from the traditional to contemporary. You may for instance choose to make a Log Cabin quilt using this much-loved pieced block pattern. It has been around for any number of years and has been made many, many times, but your choice and placement of the fabrics and blocks themselves will make the quilt unique to you. So it is with quilting designs – the individual patterns in a quilt may have been used since time immemorial (viz. the snail-creep or spiral) but they can be adapted, re-scaled and combined with other patterns to form a design which is new. If you have the opportunity to look at old quilts, you are sure to find inspiration aplenty and the aim of this chapter is to furnish you with some ideas which can be developed into your own designs.

The quilt shown opposite comes from the quilting tradition of the North East of England and is typical in its use of highly complex patterns to build up a pleasing overall design. Compare it with the texture and patterns of the quilt shown on page 129, which is a quilt from Wales. Both traditions are based on a formal structure but the patterns and designs are easily distinguishable one from the other. The Welsh patterns are simple and bold, giving a strongly sculptured texture, whereas the North East patterns are more flowing and give a deep, rich texture. Identifying specific regional characteristics of old quilts is not always an easy matter, but what is apparent in the majority of cases is an understanding of what quilting can do and what works best: that is, keep it simple both in pattern and structure, and use contrast and repetition.

Opposite: The sheen of the cotton sateen fabric and the fine quilting make this a highly covetable quilt. Quilt courtesy of Margaret Philbin.

Paper cutting

It would be possible to speculate almost endlessly about how individual quilting patterns originated and were developed, and we tend to believe that artistic ability was involved somewhere along the line. This may indeed be true (and the whole question of 'quilts as art' is thankfully not within the scope of this book) but it is just as likely that a great number of patterns found on old quilts were originated and adapted by more prosaic methods such as papercutting, classically defined many years ago by one quilter as 'worrying with scissors and brown paper'. As a means of creating patterns papercutting has much to recommend it, requiring no specialist equipment or abilities. Try it for yourself with the following simple exercises.

1   Fold a sheet of lightweight paper (typing or tracing/greaseproof is ideal) in half (Fig 1a) and cut a basic leaf shape without first marking a cutting line (Fig 1b). Fold a second sheet of paper in half, this time cutting a heart shape (Fig 1c), again without any pre-marking.

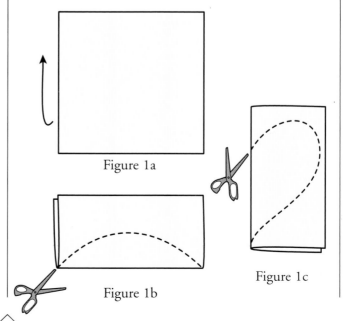

Figure 1a

Figure 1b

Figure 1c

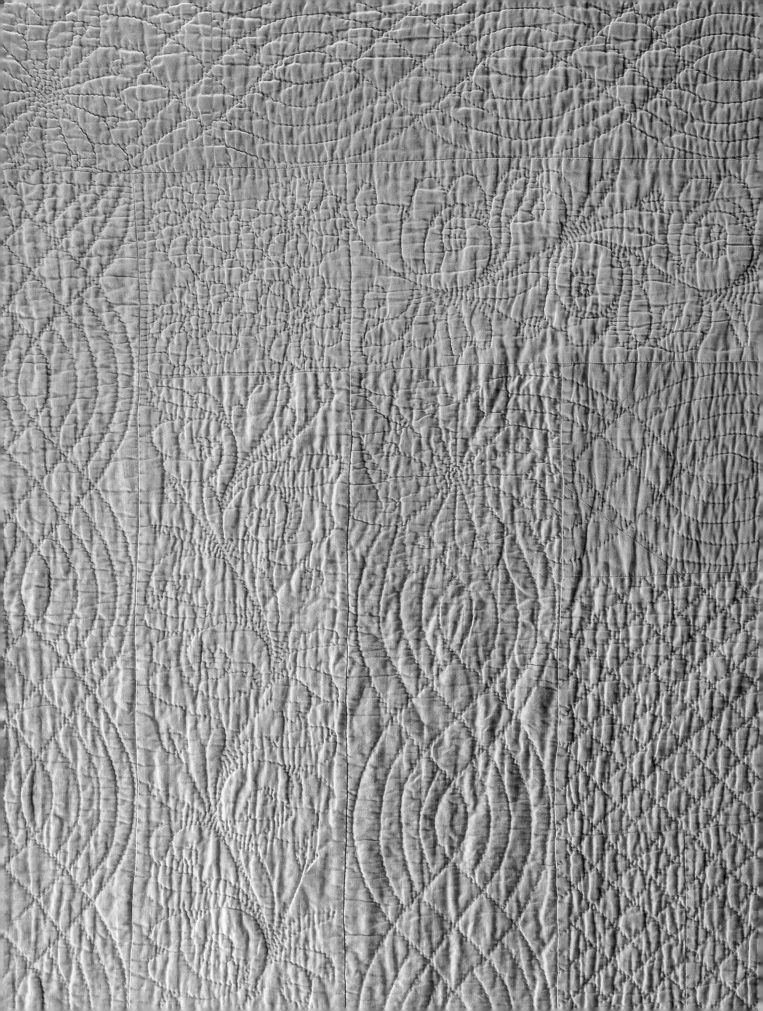

Now you have two paper templates which could be used to build up a simple design as in Figs 2a and b.

Figure 2a

Figure 2b

2   Fold a sheet of lightweight paper into quarters and using Fig 3 as a guide only, cut a simple curving line starting at A and finishing at B – notice where the fold-

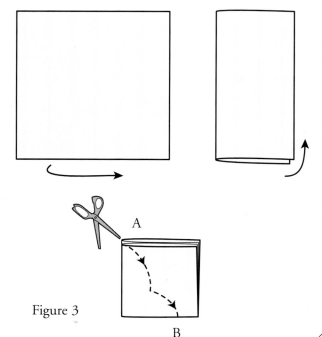

Figure 3

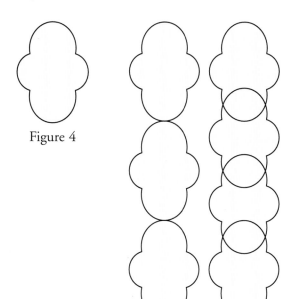

Figure 4

Figure 5

ed edges of the paper are in relation to the cutting line. Unfold your paper and the shape you have cut may well look something like Fig 4. This motif could be developed into a border or strippy pattern as in Fig 5.

3   If you feel adventurous, you could make one or two more cuts, as suggested in Fig 6, before unfolding to give a more complex pattern such as the one in Fig 7.

Figure 6

Figure 7

4 Now take a sheet of paper, fold it into eight, and cut a symmetrical curve across the wide end of the wedge as in Fig 8.

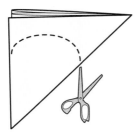

Figure 8

An easy way of achieving this curve is to use a coin to mark a line before cutting, although with a little practise you will find that cutting curves without pre-marking is not at all difficult. Unfold the cut paper. You now have the outline of one of the world's most frequently used quilting patterns. Some of its various forms are shown in Fig 9.

Figure 9

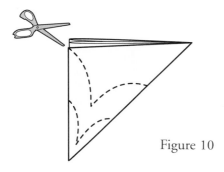

Figure 10

You can also use the 'fold into eight' method to make other motifs or patterns for quilting; a suggestion is sketched in Fig 10 for you to use as a starting point.

Remaking old quilts

You may be lucky enough to own an old quilt – why not look at it with a view to using and adapting some element of the quilting for a new project? If you lay a sheet of tracing paper on top of a quilt, you may be able to see enough of the quilting pattern through the paper to take a rough tracing which can be smoothed out and tidied up afterwards. The advent of enlarging/reducing photocopiers has made the task of re-scaling patterns virtually pain-free, but you may prefer to use the time-honoured grid method (Fig 11).

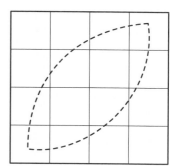

Figure 11

Designing wholecloth quilts

A few words at this point on the subject of design for wholecloth quilts. All too often 'design' is confused with 'draw'. Design means making decisions and arranging patterns or motifs into a pleasing whole, and is something all of us can do. Resist the temptation to use lots of different motifs or patterns; consider using just a few motifs but change their size or scale and add contrast with background quilting. Look at the scale of the patterns on pages 130–131 and see just how big and bold they look , even at this scale, compared with quilting patterns suitable for cushions and for spaces alongside patchwork or appliqué. It is not always a straightforward transition from one scale of pattern to another. And yet, a wholecloth quilt is not just a labour of love and exercise in superhuman patience. In fact, with no points, seams, blocks and sashings to match up, and no agonising over fabric choices, making a wholecloth quilt can be pure enjoyment.

Now a few words about precision and accuracy in drafting and marking for large-scale wholecloth quilting. Unless your only aim in life is to win umpteen blue ribbons at competitive shows, please do not let precision and accuracy overrule everything else. While both are highly commendable goals, most of us find them impossible to consistently achieve. Quilting involves that magical third dimension of texture from fabric and it is not always possible to coax fabric into behaving like paper on a drawing board. While I would not wish you to be totally oblivious to the basic precepts of accuracy, just do the best you can each time and let it go at that; a little imprecision adds a lot of charm and you will become more adept with every project.

The two projects which are presented here illustrate the main points of quilt design: simplicity, repetition and contrast. One of the quilts is 'proper' wholecloth and the other has relatively simple piecing. All of the measurements and patterns given in the following pages are taken directly from the quilts themselves and have not been 'tidied up' and made mathematically exact. I hope you will approach them with a positive spirit of adventure, looking at the large scale of the patterns and seeing how two anonymous quilters from the past approached the question of filling space simply and to good effect. If you are by nature a precise worker who needs to have everything just so, with perfect repetitions of perfect patterns, then I suggest that you use these patterns and plans as a starting point and re-draft the patterns to your liking on a Master Sheet (see page 11) before you begin.

On a practical note, when you seam together lengths of fabric to make tops and backings for large wholecloth quilts, it is preferable (and traditional) not to have a centre seam on the top of the quilt, while a centred lateral seam presents fewer problems on the back. But you do need to consider where the seams will actually fall and arrange it so that they do not coincide, which would make quilting difficult. It is better to have one full width flanked by two half widths of fabric for the top (Fig 12) and a centre lateral seam on the back (Fig 13). Alternatives for the

back would be to have either two seams (Fig 14) or a centred seam, depending on which is the most economical use of the fabric you have.

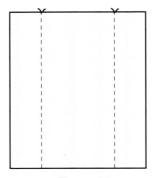

Figure 12

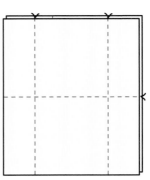

Figure 13

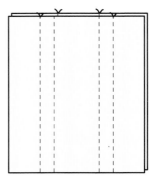

Figure 14

RED WELSH QUILT

This handsome quilt was languishing in an antique shop until one of my students came along and decided it would prefer to be in my quilt cupboard – she was so sure I'd want the quilt that she paid for it (on my behalf) there and then! Very much a case of pay first and consult later, but her judgement was absolutely correct and I was thrilled to be able to add this unbudgeted purchase to my collection. The quilt was made around the turn of the century in Anglesey, North Wales, and is in almost perfect condition, having had very little use. Both the top and backing fabrics are heavyweight twill and the batting is cotton.

YOU WILL NEED

6½ yards (6m) of fabric for the quilt top
6½ yards (6m) of backing fabric
Double-bed size pre-cut batting
Matching or contrasting thread
Quilting needles
Quilting hoop or frame
Fabric marker
Template material

Finished size: 76 inches (193cm) square

1   To wash or not to wash (your fabrics)? If you will be using cotton for the top, batting and backing, then you could give your quilt a traditional, slightly used look by quilting it first and washing it later. You may prefer to address any potential shrinkage by washing the fabrics beforehand. Preparation of battings depends very much on the type you choose; read and

Stunning colour and simple quilting patterns complement one another perfectly in this antique quilt from Anglesey, North Wales.

follow the manufacturer's recommendations carefully and remember that wool battings do not usually require any preparation (see page 9).

2 Press and seam together both top and backing fabrics to make the required size and press all the seams open.

3 Measure and mark the main design areas directly onto the quilt top using Fig 15 as a guide. Trace the pattern motifs on pages 130–133 to make templates or a Master Sheet according to your preference and choice of fabric. Fill in the framework using Fig 15 as a reference for the placement of patterns. It is not essential to follow this outline rigidly, and if you change or re-draft one or two things, you will have added your own 'handprint' to the finished quilt. You may notice that the patterns are not as mathematically precise as they appear to be on the quilt itself. The patterns were taken directly from the quilt which at

Figure 15

first glance appears to be very rigidly laid out in terms of the pattern structure. But quilting does not require the same precision as rocket science and old-time quilters had a more relaxed attitude to their work. The moral is that 'fudging' is fine so long as it is relatively discreet.

Give some thought to your choice of marker for a project of this size, which will not be completed overnight; the marker needs to be visible on the fabric and sufficiently long-lasting to survive frequent handling, as well as being relatively easy to remove when all the stitching is complete.

4   Once the quilt top is marked to your satisfaction, assemble the three quilt layers and baste

carefully. Again, you might like to fold over and baste the raw edges to protect them.

5   The original quilt is stitched with white thread, which in no way detracts from the glowing impact of the red top fabric, but you may prefer to use a matching colour. The stitching sequence can be either from the middle outwards or from one edge, but should be systematic.

6   Check that you have completed all the quilting before removing the basting stitches and deciding how you will finish the quilt edges. Sides to middle (see page 17) was used on this quilt but binding in a matching fabric would be an attractive alternative. Don't forget that all-important label.

Centre

RED WELSH QUILT PATTERNS – enlarge by 167%

RED WELSH QUILT PATTERNS – enlarge by 167%

SANDERSON STAR QUILT

This gorgeous quilt was 'rescued' from a local charity shop by a keen-eyed quilter who couldn't believe her luck in finding such a gem. Made from soft yellow and cream-coloured cotton sateen with a cotton batting, the stitching on the flowing patterns is fine and well done. The framework of the quilt is a bordered star pattern which is often referred to as a Sanderson Star, after Elizabeth Sanderson, a highly influential quilter and quilt 'stamper' (marker/designer) whose work had a considerable influence on the quilting tradition in the North East of England.

The quilting patterns used on this quilt can be found on pages 138–141. If you have a little piecing and quilting experience, a quilt such as this is well within your capabilities, but it could not be considered a quick quilt project! If time is limited but you wanted to capture some of the flavour of this quilt, you could scale down and adapt some of the patterns into your own new arrangements for a smaller project. The original quilt is made from a medium-weight sateen which has retained a lovely soft sheen over the years. You may like to use sateen also but bear in mind that it will be fractionally less easy to stitch through than a good-quality dressweight cotton. Remember that the ideal backing fabric for a quilt is one which is very similar in weight to that of the top, so make sure you buy enough. There is no reason why you should not use the patterns on pages 138–141 and the layout in Fig 16 on a single colour quilt if you prefer not to piece the star and borders first – you will still make a beautiful quilt.

Opposite: The sheen of the cotton sateen fabric and the fine quilting make this a highly covetable quilt.
Quilt courtesy of Margaret Philbin.

YOU WILL NEED

3 yards (2.75m) of each of two colours of fabric for the quilt top
6 yards (5.5m) of backing fabric
Double-bed or king-size pre-cut batting – you might like to try one of the new lighter-weight cottons
Quilting thread to tone with your fabrics
Fabric marker
Basting thread
Quilting hoop or frame
Template material and tracing paper OR sufficient tracing paper to make a one-quarter size pattern
Sewing machine for piecing the quilt top

Finished size: 82 x 87 inches (208 x 220cm)

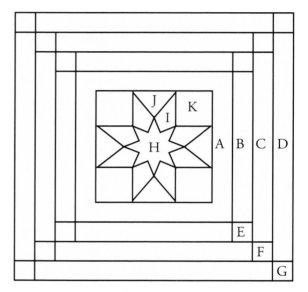

Figure 16

Border A	=	cross hatch	measures 7¾ in (20cm)
Border B	=	cable	measures 6½ in (16cm)
Border C	=	floral scroll	measures 6¼ in (15.5cm)
Border D	=	cable	measures 6 in (15cm)
Square E	=	pattern E	
Square F	=	pattern F	
Square G	=	pattern E	

1   To misquote the immortal words of the famous Mrs Beaton, 'first piece your quilt top'. The templates for the central star are given on page 140. These are shown without seam allowances and you will need to add an allowance of your choice to all sides of each of the templates before cutting them out. It may be advisable to have this seam allowance on the generous

BORDERS B AND D – cable

BORDER C – Floral scroll

SANDERSON STAR QUILT PATTERNS – enlarge by 166%

BORDERS B AND D – cable

side to give maximum flexibility for piecing. The centre star is cut as one complete piece rather than in diamond sections – a liberal application of spray starch to your fabric will keep it stable and make it easier to handle. Figs 17, 18 and 19 show the construction sequence for the star and borders. While the star can be stitched by hand or machine, the long border seams will be finished more quickly if done by machine.

Note: The first inside border A (see Fig 16, page 134) measures 7¾ inches (20cm), the second border B measures 6½ inches (16cm), the third border C is 6¼ inches (15.5cm) and the final outside border D is 6 inches (15cm). In fact, border A has two different

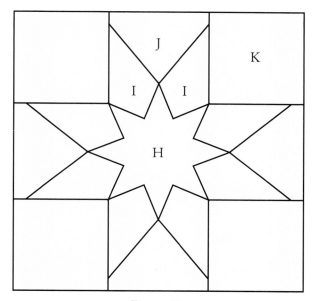

Figure 17

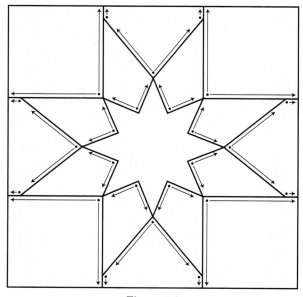

Figure 18

measurements on the original quilt. At the sides it is 7¾ inches (20cm) and at the top and bottom it is only 4 inches (10cm).

2   Decide whether or not to pre-wash your fabrics, then take the appropriate steps before measuring and cutting out your fabrics accurately, bearing in mind that other well-worn adage: 'measure twice and cut once'. It is advisable to piece the entire top first and then use these measurements as a guide to assist you when you are making up the backing fabric, which must be at least 2 inches (5cm) larger than the top on all sides. Take time and care when pressing the seams of both the top and the backing of the quilt so that both are as smooth as possible.

It was only when I came to work out the measurements and quilting patterns and began to calculate the yardage for this quilt that I realised how much it had been 'fudged'. The star points do not all meet perfectly or sharply, the two yellow cable borders have been pieced together from some very odd-angled lengths of fabric, and the crosshatching drifts off line in several places. Of course you are not compelled to follow suit, and I'm sure you will take even greater pains with all aspects of the quiltmaking process, but it is interesting nonetheless to find that such a lovely quilt has a number of endearing imperfections.

The shapes (on page 141) which complete the star are larger than the star points themselves so that, as you will see from Figs 18 and 19, there are a number of short set-in seams. We would perhaps expect the star points, triangles and squares to fit each other so that the star points are right at the edge of the block. It may be that working with larger squares and triangles

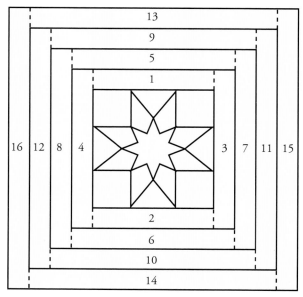

Figure 19

means that any discrepancies at the points are rather less obvious and they give the impression that the star is floating on the background. The quilter responsible for this lovely quilt went one stage further in making the star float by making her first border the same colour as the star background and continuing the crosshatching out from the squares and triangles into this border.

3 Construct the backing fabric after you have taken the measurements of the completed top – hopefully these will not be too far adrift from those given above! Press the seams open before pressing the whole backing and laying it out somewhere as flat as possible to avoid creasing.

4 The quilting patterns for this quilt are on pages 136 and 138–140 indicates their placement. Trace the patterns to make templates for marking directly onto the fabric, or make a Master Sheet which is a full quarter of the whole quilt. A compromise might be to use the pattern tracings to make a Master Sheet for each of the main quilt areas such as first border, second border, etc. You might find this a more manageable way of marking if you are using the trace-through method. Decide if the crosshatching or grid lines for the background areas should be marked before or after you begin quilting. If you opt for before, take care that your marking (and measuring) is as accurate as possible and that you do not drag the fabric out of true as

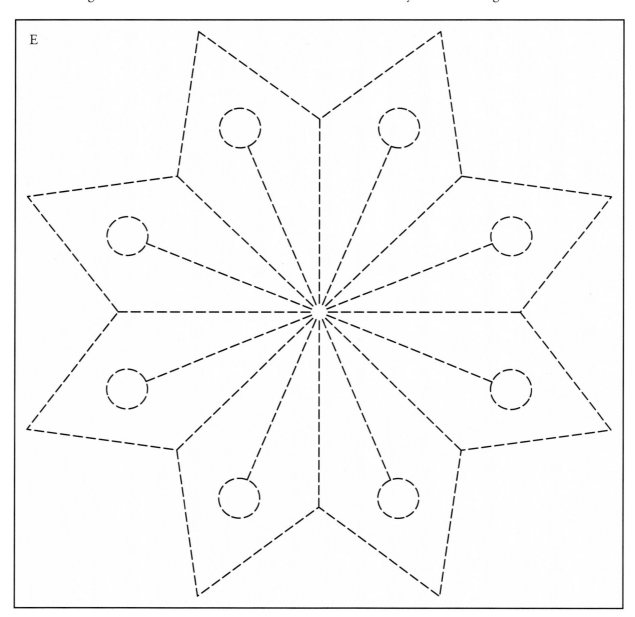

SANDERSON STAR QUILTING PATTERNS – enlarge by 166%

you mark the pattern. It may be as easy to use masking tape (see pages 10–11) to mark out the guide lines when you are ready to quilt these areas. On the original antique quilt the crosshatched lines are 1 inch (2.5cm) apart.

5   There is no denying that basting a quilt of this size is a tedious process, but it has to be done. With a positive attitude (and a little help from your friends or family), it could be over before the pain gets too excruciating.

6   By now you will be familiar with the fact that quilting can begin at the centre of the quilt and radiate outwards, or from one edge to the other back and forth. Decide which sequence you will follow and

begin. If you need another wise saying to help you on your way, remember the Chinese proverb of the journey of a thousand miles beginning with just one step... The process of quilting is (or should be) as enjoyable as the finished product; remember that it is not a race against the clock. Savour the process, set yourself an easily achieved stint to do each day if you must, but above all enjoy and take pride in what you are stitching.

7   The customary finish on a quilt of this type was sides to middle (see page 17), with the stitching often done by machine, which was considered to be a stronger and therefore superior stitch. (In the infancy of the sewing machine, a machine finish on a quilt

F

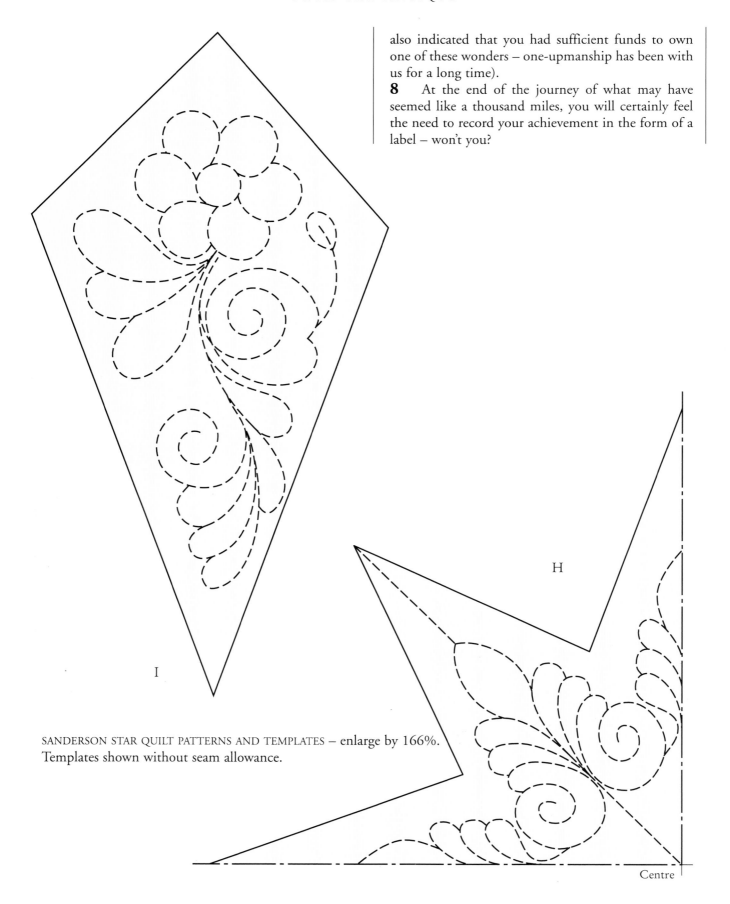

also indicated that you had sufficient funds to own one of these wonders – one-upmanship has been with us for a long time).

8   At the end of the journey of what may have seemed like a thousand miles, you will certainly feel the need to record your achievement in the form of a label – won't you?

SANDERSON STAR QUILT PATTERNS AND TEMPLATES – enlarge by 166%.
Templates shown without seam allowance.

I

H

Centre

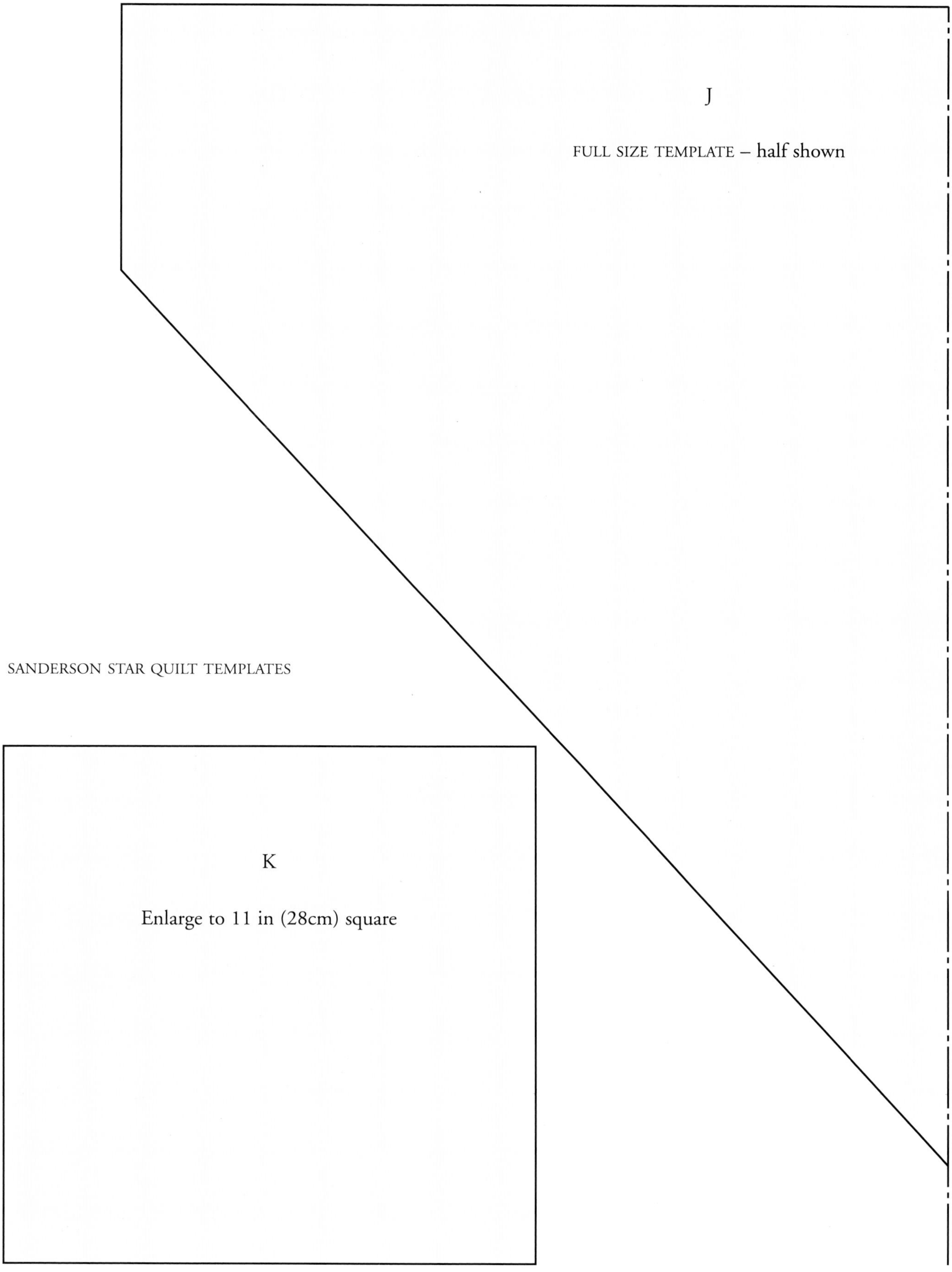

J

FULL SIZE TEMPLATE – half shown

SANDERSON STAR QUILT TEMPLATES

K

Enlarge to 11 in (28cm) square

SELECTED BIBLIOGRAPHY

Note: The following list is by no means exhaustive or comprehensive, but has been chosen to augment the information and techniques presented in this book.

The Essential Quilter
Barbara Chainey
David and Charles
1993

The Ins and Outs:
Perfecting the Quilting Stitch
Patricia Morris
American Quilters Society
1990

Quilting with Style
Gwen Marston and Joe
Cunningham
American Quilters Society
1993

The Quilt Design Sourcebook
Dorothy Osler
That Patchwork Place
1996

Trapunto and Stippling
John Flynn
Flynn Quilt Frame Co
1992

Happy Endings
Mimi Dietrich
That Patchwork Place
1988

The Art of Kantha Embroidery
Niaz Zaman
University Press Ltd
(1981) 1993

Trapunto Quilting
Hari Walner
C & T Publishing
1996

Machine Quilting Made Easy
Maurine Noble
That Patchwork Place
1994

Quilting Makes the Quilt
Lee Cleland
That Patchwork Place
1994

Sashiko, Blue and White Art
of Japan
Mende & Morishige
Shufonotomo
1991

Sashiko and Beyond
Saikoh Takano
Chilton
1993

ACKNOWLEDGEMENTS

This book represents the triumph of persistent nagging over prolonged procrastination. For their unflagging patience, understanding and forbearance I owe a considerable debt to all of the following:

Personal and inspirational

Derek, who always remains calm, positive and practical in the face of adversity and hysteria, Anna who, through force of circumstance, is now an accomplished cook and has learned to drive, and my mother, who lives in hope of seeing my home clean and tidy just once in her lifetime. To Patricia, Chris, Cath, Pat and Mike, Maggie and Alan, Elaine, Joy, Roberts Reliable Reservations, Margaret and George, Jean-Ann, Lynne, Sem and Bridget, Jacquie and Denzil – thanks for everything.

The editorial team

At David and Charles, Cheryl Brown, Jane Trollope, and Brenda Morrison. Maggi McCormick has once again worked her magic, coaxing and cajoling text, diagrams and pictures into a coherent whole. The indefatigable Roger Brown was challenged to 'photograph these and make them all look wonderful' yet kept his sense of humour and perspective throughout the entire proceedings as well as meeting the challenge. Thanks also to Michael Servian at KJD.

Loans

Di Clarke, Sandie Lush, Margaret Philbin, Patricia Cox, Lynne Williams and Sue Longhurst obligingly passed over quilts and precious pieces of work without knowing exactly when these would be seen again and I thank them for their trust and generosity.

Practical stitching

Ann Jermey, Sally Radway, Sandie Lush, Marian Chainey and Maggie Alexander all did heroic stints of quilting and sewing at short notice and often to very tight deadlines – currently none of them are returning my calls in fear they may be persuaded to get involved in something similar. I am extremely grateful to each of them.

I have greatly missed my good friend Ken Goodwin during the preparation of this book. Ken brought a practical, lively interest and good humour to everything he undertook. The excellent illustrations he provided for *The Essential Quilter* were, sadly, his last major project.

INDEX

Page numbers in *italics* indicate illustrations.

All over designs, 96
Antique quilts, patterns from, *123,* 125, 127–41, *127, 129, 135*
Appliqué, 94–7, *95, 101,* 117–21, *117, 119;* enhancement of by quilting, 97

Background quilting, 96–7
Basting, 11, 65; gun, 12, 65
Batting, 9, 64
Bed quilt projects, 35–41, *36, 72–3,* 108–13, *109,* 127–33, *127, 129,* 134–41, *135*
Beeswax, 12
Big stitch quilting, 93
Binding, 17–18
Borders, 16

Chain piecing, 98
Christmas Wallhanging, 114–16, *115*
Continuous line patterns, 64–5
Corded quilting, 50–3, *51, 57, 58, 61*
Crib quilt projects, 42–5, *43,* 46–9, *47, 51,* 72–5
Crosshatch quilting, 96, 97, 113
Cushion, making up, 20; projects, *23,* 28–34, *29–34,* 56–62, 67–9, *69,* 76–8, *77,* 81–4, *83,* 92–3, *92,* 99–101, *101, 117,* 118–21, *119*

Darning foot, 64
Design, 24, 125–6

Equipment *see* Tools

Fabric, 8, 22, 64, 90
Feathered square, 108–13
Finishing, 16–21
Flying geese, 102–10, *103*
Frames, 13–14
Free machine quilting, 66, *69*

Georgian Geese *see* Flying geese
Grid *see* Crosshatch quilting

Hand quilting, 22–7, *23,* 28–49, *29–34, 37, 43, 47*
Hanging quilts *see* Sleeve
Hoop, 13–14

Indian quilting *see* Kantha work
Invisible thread, 64
Ironing *see* Pressing
Italian quilting *see* Corded quilting

Kantha work, 90–3, *91, 92*

Labels, 21
Laundering *see* Washing quilts

Machine quilting, 15, 63–78, *69, 71, 72–3, 77,* 99–101, *101, 103,* 104–5
Marking, patterns, 9, 52, 65; tools, 9
Masking tape, 9
Master sheet, 10
Meander quilting, 66, *71,* 97
Mitred corners, 16–17
Motifs, quilting, 96

Needles, hand, 12, 79, 90; machine, 12, 64

Outline quilting, *103,* 105, 108–13, *109*

Paper cutting, 122–5
Patchwork, 94–116, *95, 101, 103, 109*
Patterns, quilting, 10, 22, 50, 64
Piping, 19–20
Practice piece, 65
Pressing, 20, 98
Projects, crib quilt, 42–5, *43,* 46–9, *47,* 72–5; cushions, *23,* 28–34, *29–34,* 56–62, 67–9, *69,* 76–8, 81–4, 92–3, 99–102, *117,* 118–21, *119;* full size quilt, 127–33, *127, 129,* 134–41, *135;* single quilt, 35–41, *36,* 72–5, *72–3,* 108–13, *109;* strippy quilt, *36,* 53–41, 72–5, *72–3;* table runner, *83,* 85–9; waistcoat, 70–7,

71; wallhanging, 85–9, 102–7, 114–16, *115*

Quick piecing, 108–13, 114–16

Rotary cutter, 8

Safety pins, 12, 65
Sanderson, Elizabeth, 134; Star Quilt, 134–41, *135*
Sashiko quilting, 79–89, *83;* Table Runner, 85–9, *83*
Scissors, 8
Scribble cloth *see* Practice piece
Sewing machine, 63–4
Sleeve, 21
Spinning Star Cushion, 99–101, *101*
Stencils, 10
Stipple quilting, 54–5
Stitch, and tear, 11; for corded quilting, 51–3; kantha work, 90; machine, 66; quilting, 15, 24–7; sashiko, 80; size of, 27; stab, 15, 46, 96
Strippy quilt projects, 35–41, *36–7,* 72–5, *72–3*

Table runner, *83,* 85–9
Tacking *see* Basting
Tacking gun *see* Basting gun
Templates, 10
Tension, machine stitch, 64
Thimbles, 12
Thread, corded work, 52; kantha, 90; machine, 64; quilting, 12; sashiko, 79
Tools, 8–14, 22
Trapunto, 53–4, *51, 57, 58, 61*

Wadding *see* Batting
Waistcoat, 70–1, *71*
Walking foot, 64
Wallhanging, 85–9, 102–7; Christmas, 114–16, *115*
Washing quilts, 20–1
Welsh quilt, 127–33, *127, 129*

Yarn, for cording, 52

1. Books may be kept two weeks and may be renewed
once for the same period, except 7 day books, magazines
and reserved items.

2. A fine is charged for each day a book is not returned
according to the above rule. No book will be issued to any
person incurring such a fine until it has been paid.

3. All injuries to books beyond reasonable wear and all
losses shall be made good to the satisfaction of the
Librarian.

4. Each borrower is held responsible for all items
charged on his card and for all fines accruing on the
same

APR 1 2 1999

GAYLORD M